Moses on Leadership

*How to Become a Great Leader
in Forty Short Years*

Dr. Gene Mims

KINGSTONE MEDIA

Published by Bay Forest Books
An Imprint of Kingstone Media Group
P.O. Box 491600
Leesburg, FL 34749-1600
www.bayforestbooks.com

Printed in the United States of America by
Bay Forest Books

Library of Congress Cataloguing-in-Publication Data is on file.

ISBN 978-1-61328-029-4

I joyfully dedicate this book to …

*…Ann, my wife and best friend, who brings joy
and balance to me;*

*…Jeff, Kathy, Marianne, and Justin, children by birth
and marriage, who are blessings;*

*…Sara Kate, Hampton, and Margie, three delightful
people, who make me want to live well;*

*…the people of Judson Baptist Church, who called me
to return to my calling;*

*…the staff at Judson Baptist Church, who make
Kingdom work so much fun.*

Table of Contents

Preface

—◦◦◦—

Of all the characters in Scripture, Moses nearly stands alone after Jesus Christ. His life and writings are the foundations of Old Testament history, law, theology, ethics, social constructs, and many other developments in world history. Nations have based legal systems and moral codes on his work. The Ten Commandments are arguably the most recognized religious document in the world. His name is easily recognized in major religions outside of Jewish and Christian groups.

We actually know little about him personally. Things like his size, stature, or personal characteristics are left to our imaginations or to some distant recall of Charlton Heston in the movie, *The Ten Commandments*. What we do know of Moses we learn from Scripture, especially the first five books attributed to him. His call from God to lead the children of Israel out of bondage in Egypt into the Promised Land is a fundamental part of our knowledge of God, His people, and His redemptive purposes. Without Moses there would be no narrative to excite us and to show us the character of our God in the early years of our tradition.

The various experiences that Moses had both personally and as a leader serve us well as we study them. One thing that stands out among his many characteristics and experiences is his leadership. It is no small feat to lead any nation or large group of people. But to deliver them from slavery, to wander in a wilderness with them for forty years, building their very fabric as people, to write their theological history, deliver their book of faith and practice, and finally to prepare them to possess a land God had chosen to give them is almost incomprehensible.

Most national leaders are elected to leadership in nations that already have legal codes, economies, armies, educational and social institutions. They may have to lead their nations through times of war, famine, economic downturns, and social unrest, but they start with *something*. Moses had neither the luxury of an entity to begin with nor any time or training to get ready for the task. His rise to leadership began with a frightening call from God through a burning bush. God called him to an impossible task filled with risks and dangers. God chose to send him to Pharaoh and demand the release of all the Hebrews.

Whatever he might have experienced in Egypt before he ran away could not have prepared him to do what God had chosen for him. There was no wilderness school of leadership to matriculate from and no mentor to prepare his mind and heart for what lay ahead; just a call to come and a command to go.

May I confess to you as we begin this journey together that Moses' story stirs wonder and passion in me? I, like most of you reading this book, have been a leader for many years. I have read about great leaders. I have studied a variety of ministry, military, business, political, and educational leaders. I have given most of my life to leading people. It's what leaders do. But I discovered some great leadership principles detailed by Moses' life in the book of Exodus—principles that I had not noticed before. Some of these principles are similar to those found in the lives and works of other great leaders, but some are not. When they are all taken together they render a unique set of principles that encourage and guide leaders in all types of circumstances.

I write these insights from the perspective of a Christian leader. I offer no apology for that as sadly many leaders do today. I have been in ministry for forty years serving as a pastor, a corporate vice-president of a large denominational entity, and president of a small start-up ministry. So I write from a personal history that might seem unique to you. At my heart, however, I am a pastor. In my pilgrimage I have labored with balance sheets, inventories, marketing issues, information technology developments, human resource problems, and the lack of capital and funding for a new start-up. I have faced the stress of buying companies, the futility of many strategic planning sessions, corporate politics, and a thousand other business issues. But I am a pastor—so while I have business experience, my greatest satisfaction is leading God's people to make His name known through Christ among the nations.

My issues now center in helping people and equipping them to fulfill the Great Commission. I constantly think about how to lead people to join God in His great redeeming work. I have traded corporate reports for church statistics and products for relationships.

I have to disclose, however, that what I have learned from Moses' leadership journey began for me in a corporate setting where I faced all the issues any business faces today. Thankfully, I got to do some speaking, preaching, and serving as interim pastor along the way. While the beginning of this journey started in one place it has come with me to another. As the Psalmist wrote,

> *"The lines have fallen to me in pleasant places; indeed my heritage is beautiful to me."* (Psalm 16:6)

So I reiterate that I write as a Christian leader without apology. Truths about leadership come from many sources, but Moses is different. It is disappointing that so many Christian leadership resources parrot secular business and management leaders with a little spiritual flavor put in to meet a market demand. I can attest that business leadership and Kingdom leadership, while having many similarities, are *very* different. Our leadership comes through a relationship with Christ, a call to serve the Father as one of His leaders, and a commission to join Him in Kingdom work. What may happen on Wall Street or at a corporate headquarters is interesting and important but not normative for Christian leaders.

If I have written what I have truly learned, then you will be encouraged as you take this short journey with me. I hope we can laugh together, learn together, and celebrate our callings as Kingdom leaders. I pray that God has given me insights that will help you and that they will be multiplied through your life as you make your own discoveries and become a better leader. In other words, I hope you get your own personal blessing from the discoveries I have made in this remarkable life of Moses.

There is one fundamental truth that we discover in Moses' experience, namely, *that it takes a long time to become a great leader.* So let's get started and wander around with Moses for forty years to see if God has some other leadership truths for us to discover.

Chapter One

—◦◦◦—

The Leader's Call

"And she named him Moses; because I drew him out of the water."
(Exodus 2:10)

"And Moses was one hundred and twenty years old when he died."
(Deuteronomy 34:7)

I want to start out with one of the most important principles that we glean from Moses' life and work, namely, *that it takes a long time to become a great leader.* There are exceptions, but you and I are not those exceptions or we would not be enjoying this Mosaic journey together. So, if you can get this into your thinking right away, it will be helpful. Moses' experience in leadership began fast but developed over forty years.

The Hebrews had endured slavery in Egypt since the days of Joseph's passing. His story is remarkable in itself as he rose from slavery to national leadership, saving his family and all of Egypt from severe famine. His vision, wisdom, and leadership were instrumental in the rise of Egypt as a world power and Pharaoh as a complete sovereign in Egypt.

But time marches forward and in time there were leaders in Egypt who knew nothing of Joseph but knew a lot about the Hebrews. The Hebrews had grown in number to become a threatening menace to a succession of leaders and pharaohs in Egypt. Great in numbers did not translate to strong in influence for the Hebrews, so they were enslaved to labor for and under pharaohs who followed one another in leadership.

It was to this national condition that Moses was born. His mother gave birth to him just at a time when Pharaoh decreed to all the Hebrew midwives that males born to Hebrew women were to be killed at birth. Moses' mother determined to save his life by hiding him in a basket and floating him in the reeds along the Nile River. His sister was charged to watch him and protect him from harm.

One day Pharaoh's daughter and her maidservants were bathing in the river when she saw the basket. She dispatched a maid to retrieve it and discovered Moses lying inside. Immediately his sister intervened for him, offering the services of a Hebrew woman to nurse him until he was weaned. The woman of course was Moses' own mother. Pharaoh's daughter agreed to the plan and later brought him to her home and to Pharaoh's court.

Scripture gives only a sketch of his early life but we learn that Moses was raised as other young men in Pharaoh's house. He would have been well regarded, well fed, well educated, and in general given a life of rich future promise in Egypt.

We know that did not happen in Egypt. Moses saw an Egyptian beating a Hebrew slave one day and in anger he killed the Egyptian. He hid the body thinking no one saw what had happened. Later when two Hebrews were fighting, Moses tried to intercede. One challenged him, asking if he would kill one of them as he had the Egyptian. Moses realized that his crime was now public and, to make matters worse, Pharaoh had learned of it and had issued a warrant to kill him. In panic he fled to the Midianite wilderness.

These events are recorded in Exodus in rapid fashion, without much detail, in order that the real story can be given. That story involves Moses, Pharaoh, armies, plagues, deaths, and many other events that make the story of Moses both real and important.

Whatever we make of Moses' desire to assist his fellow Hebrews, his murder of the Egyptian was wrong. It destroyed his future and security and off to the wilderness he ran, not to develop his life but simply to save it. His options were few, his problems many, and his future seemed bleak.

We will learn that in time, however, God had plans for him. A good leadership lesson happens right here. *Our personal failures do not always mean the end of our leadership.* God was not through with Moses despite the murder he committed. He had a long eventful life ahead of him in God's service.

Moses was never going to lead in Egypt but Egypt was not the only place God needed leaders. We have to remember a number of important things as Christian leaders, namely:

1. Leaders make mistakes, sin, fail, and can lose their way. These things happen to all leaders, even to the men and women God calls to do His work.

2. Leaders can be removed from one Kingdom assignment and used by God in something else. You may have done something to lose what you love to do for the Lord but God will use you if you trust Him, repent of sins and failures, and seek Him to serve Him wherever He sends you, to do whatever He desires. Loving God is first; serving Him comes next.

3. Remember that your call from God was to Himself. What He first called you to do followed your call to enter a relationship with Him.

4. Sins, failures, and seasons of loss are things that God uses to build our lives and characters. Focus on your relationship with Him and your leadership will grow stronger during these times.

No one with reason would suggest that sins, failures, and mistakes are good things for us. We can be forgiven for every sin but the circumstances those sins create are sometimes with us for the rest of our lives. But through forgiveness we can learn from our mistakes and we can humble ourselves before the Lord, asking Him to restore us in His service. Your leadership location may change but your call to leadership will not. Your leadership circumstance may change but your usefulness to God will not.

I have experienced this very principle personally. I have learned from my sins and mistakes over the forty years of my ministry that although those mistakes were damaging to my life and leadership, through confessing my sins, I have been restored by God to lead His people again.

LEADERSHIP FOR A LONG TIME

Many of us are under such pressure as leaders that we have only a short view of our lives and the time we will spend leading God's people. The reason it takes a long time to become a great leader is that it takes a long time for God to work His will in His people. God's people, like their leaders, don't get everything the first time around. It takes time. In fact, time is one of our best resources. Leaders do not grow up overnight. They don't know much when they begin. They haven't been around long enough to understand what life is about and how to navigate through the twists and turns of circumstances, mistakes, and challenges, to say nothing of God-sized assignments.

When we look at Moses' life and work it seems as though he went through four definable stages in his leadership journey. Each stage was different because the circumstances called for different leadership. Each stage builds upon the one before as the leader is built into greater effectiveness.

1. Stage one was an orientation to what God wanted him to do. Moses sees a bush burning and from it the Lord unveils His plan to deliver the Israelites from Pharaoh and Egypt. Moses considers this announcement with renewed interest when he learns that God has chosen him to be His leader and spokesman. He has to deal with this radical change in his life.

2. Stage two is the trial-and-error stage. In this part of his life, Moses must organize himself and address his message to the Israelites and to Pharaoh. He has to begin doing what God has commanded. His initial efforts are met with less than stellar results. He is mocked by Pharaoh and ignored by the Israelites.

3. Stage three is where he actually leads the children of Israel out of Egypt through the Red Sea. He has successfully delivered them but now he has to deal with a new set of issues and circumstances. His leadership develops and changes to meet the new demands.

4. Stage four is the final chapter in Moses' life and leadership. He has successfully moved the Israelites from slavery to a nation ready to enter the Promised Land. His leadership in this stage is focused on preparing the people to enter the land and to prepare the next generation of leaders for their coming tasks.

LEADERSHIP BEGINNINGS

Christian leadership begins with a call from God to join Him in a task or movement. It may be a call to preach, to teach, or to begin a ministry or a business. It generally involves at least the following:

* A surprising encounter with the Lord—like a burning bush!

* A personal crisis over what God wants you to do—"You want me to do *what*?"

* An intense time of wrestling with God and His will—"I don't think I can do this."

* A final surrender to God's will and the initial attempts to do what He commands.

I would like to give you a key leadership principle that you probably already know since you are already a leader. It is this: *God never calls us to anything small*. If He did, we would do it and not give it much thought. But when God speaks and moves, it is always something big.

Can you recall the last time God spoke to you about what He wanted you to do? Can you ever forget it?

When the Lord called me to preach, I was sixteen years old and relatively clueless about anything to do with the Kingdom. I had some dreams, however. I dreamed of coaching or perhaps a career in law. I thought about going to college then perhaps to graduate school then settling into a comfortable life. I could imagine marrying and having children while living close to my parents and friends in my hometown.

One January night I was in bed listening as I did each night to a faraway radio station playing my favorite songs when the Lord spoke clearly to me. I do not think it was audible but I heard it clearly in my mind. He simply said, *"You will preach for Me."* I took the earbud out and thought about what had just happened when I heard the voice again and He said the same thing. I don't know about your experiences at sixteen but nothing, and I mean nothing, like this had ever happened to me.

I pondered what I had just heard and immediately began to reason with the Lord what I was willing to do for Him. I remember pledging (with real sincerity) that I would be a Sunday School director even though I had no idea what that meant. Or, I promised, to be a deacon and even a Sunday School teacher. I may have offered my services for other spiritual offices but I was so shaken that I cannot remember anything else. I do remember that I heard the Lord's voice for a third time, not asking, not suggesting, not offering but stating plainly, *"You will preach for Me."*

Now you may think that a call to preach is not much pressure (unless you have ever faced it), but I promise you that for a sixteen-year-old it was almost too much to handle. I was willing to do anything

I could feel comfortable doing. I was unwilling to do anything that resembled a God-sized task.

Years later when I read the account of Moses with the eyes of a "called" servant of the Lord, I had great appreciation for what he went through.

> *"And the angel of the Lord appeared to him in a blazing fire from the midst of a bush; and he looked, and behold, the bush was burning with fire, yet the bush was not consumed."*
> (Exodus 3:2)

The call of God can and usually does come from the most unexpected places. For Abraham it was in a word, for Isaac it was a dream, for David it was from the anointing by a prophet, for Isaiah it was a vision, for Ezekiel a dream, for Peter a command from Christ to follow, and for Paul a blinding experience on the Damascus road.

God's call is generally verbal, specific, and frightening! In Moses' case, he no doubt had seen bushes burning due to spontaneous combustion in the heat of the wilderness. But this time the bush did not burn itself out. It kept burning and from within it a voice called Moses by name. *"Moses, Moses,"* the voice from the bush cried out. Moses responded simply by saying, "Here I am." He would later hear similar words from God when He learned that the voice in the bush was none other than the Lord God Himself.

Moses approaches the bush and is told to take his sandals off, for the ground he stood upon was holy. Then God identified Himself as the God of Abraham, Isaac, and Jacob. Moses was overwhelmed and hid his face from such a confrontation. God then goes on to say that He has seen the affliction of the Hebrews and has come to save them. I'm sure that at this point Moses must have begun to feel better with the news that his people would be delivered from Pharaoh. Not only that but they would be brought to "a land flowing with milk and honey." What news!, and Moses the Hebrew, the shepherd, the fugitive, was the first to hear of it.

I have always wondered if, as the Lord spoke to Moses, he began to wonder why he of all persons was hearing such news in such a dramatic way. Did he think that God was informing him of this to relieve his fear of being sought and found by Pharaoh? Did he imagine at first that he was dreaming and the bush was a mirage? At some point did he begin to realize that this good news came with a hidden "clincher"?

We do not know what Moses was thinking at this point but eventually the Lord told Moses that although He would deliver His people, He would use Moses as the human instrument. The words must have been staggering,

> *"Therefore, come now, and I will send you to Pharaoh, so that*
> *you may bring My people, the sons of Israel, out of Egypt."*
> (Exodus 3:10)

These words reveal truths that all of God's leaders either recognize or will discover eventually. God is constantly working in this world to establish His Kingdom purposes and He works through humans to accomplish those purposes.

In addition, while many leaders have a desperate desire for the Lord to work His purposes, they rarely see themselves as a part of the solutions God reveals. Also, it is true that while most Kingdom leaders want to lead, they rarely envision leading in the ways God requires. I have little doubt that Moses desired to help his people. I believe the news of God's plan to deliver the Hebrews from Egypt must have pleased him also. But it is easy to see from his reaction to the Lord's words that he did not see himself in the role of a deliverer.

Leadership for most people (even leaders) is theoretical or at best limited. We who lead often think our dreams and visions are grand. We can get excited about what we imagine we can do for the Lord. It seems so real, so bold and appealing. Then…God speaks to us of His plans and things change quickly. Our confidence in ourselves melts away, fear begins to grip our minds, and we, like Moses, look for ways to escape God's call.

A Big Vision and a Reluctant Leader

I often hear Christian leaders talk about vision, dreams, strategies, and goals. And frankly, most of the time I'm impressed with the size, scope, and reach of these desires. I'm generally the one in the room who feels inadequate because I don't have such plans. Yet when I can get away and think about what I have heard or seen, I realize that all these things are small compared to what God is doing in the world. God's vision is to use us to make much of Him. To reach every person with the Gospel, to evangelize them, to disciple the ones He saves, to plant churches, to start Kingdom movements, to overcome hatred, threats, and hardships as we serve Him.

None of God's plans are small, none are anything less than such as will build His Kingdom, defeat evil, and redeem persons. Given what we face in every corner of the world today, this seems daunting. But ours is not to create visions for God but to fulfill God's vision for the Kingdom.

When God calls a leader, He calls that leader to tasks that cannot be comprehended except through faith and cannot be done without His power and authority. To go against the Evil One, thrones, principalities, and powers with *our* schemes and visions is to fail. If we are content with doing what we can do, we will never see and do what only God can accomplish.

No matter what God calls you to, it will be formidable. It will take your breath away because you will quickly realize that in your power it cannot be done.

I often think of Adoniram Judson, the first American international missionary. He was brilliant beyond his peers, and had a focus that few believers ever possess. When he went to Burma with a wife, limited funds, and a Bible, he was likely to fail. But God had called him to evangelize the Burmese and despite his struggles, suffering, tortures, and pain, he stayed. He translated Scripture into their language, wrote their first dictionary, led persons to Christ, and left a legacy behind at his death that continues today. I recently received a letter from his great, great grandson congratulating us on our church's one-hundredth anniversary. As I read it I marveled at how one man with God's vision for a nation can do amazing things.

God knows what He wants done, who He wants to do it, and how it will be accomplished. His vision, once stated, may frighten us but by faith nothing can stop us from seeing it through.

MOSES, THE RELUCTANT LEADER

The excuses Moses gives to the Lord explaining why he cannot lead the Israelites out of Egypt are priceless. In fact, I imagine that most of us have used them or similar ones in our leadership journeys. Let's examine them to understand why they are actually not relevant to anything God wants to accomplish through us.

Excuse #1: I Am a Nobody.

"But Moses said to God, 'Who am I that I should bring the sons of Israel out of Egypt?'"

(Exodus 3:11)

When you face a God-sized task, it does not take long to feel inadequate. The inadequacy we face has several dimensions. One dimension is moral. Isaiah said he was unclean when he saw the Lord and was called to prophesy to the nation. Another dimension is a lack of experience like Jeremiah sensed when God called him. Amos felt inadequate because he lacked a prophetic pedigree. Peter remembered his failure and thought he might not love the Lord enough. Paul thought of himself as one born late and the least of the Apostles.

The closer we get to the task God has for us, the closer we move toward God Himself. Inadequacy is not just a feeling; it is a reality.

We are not equal to our Lord. We are not able to do anything for Him that He could not do Himself or through someone else. But He delights in calling us and using us to accomplish His purposes and to reveal His glory.

God's answer comforted and strengthened Moses. *"Certainly I will be with you"* (3:12). The reality of God's call to us is not the task alone. It is the relationship we have with Him as we do the task. He assures Moses of His presence by telling Moses that he will be successful and one day will worship with the Hebrews on the very mountain where he stands.

In effect when Moses says, *"I am a nobody,"* God says, *"You may be nobody but I am somebody and I am going with you in this task."* The God of the Universe spoke to Moses and He was going with Him to accomplish the deliverance of the sons of Israel; there was not a doubt about it happening.

Excuse #2: I Don't Know Enough.

Moses realizes that he is about to risk his life to go before Pharaoh, but he is also about to go to the Hebrews who don't know him. He imagines as he tells them that *"the God of your fathers has sent me to you,"* that they will ask His name. Moses, so far, is talking to an unidentified bush! What is the name of the One who speaks to Him about deliverance? Who is this One who promises to go with him in this task? He does not know Him and he does not know His name. If he cannot reveal the name of the One who sent him, then how will the people believe what he is saying? It is one thing to have an experience with a God no one knows; it is another to have credibility with the people He sends you to serve.

God reveals His name as, *"I AM WHO I AM"* (3:14). He says to Moses that when the question arises he is to say, *"'I AM' sent me to you."* That name means more than any of us will ever know. It has dimensions that cannot be fathomed by human minds but it is simple enough to assure every Christian leader that the Lord will be to us whatever we require in every part of our lives. The longer we know the Lord, the longer we serve Him, and the longer we seek Him the more the name means.

When Moses pleads ignorance of the One who speaks to him, he says in effect, *"I don't know enough."* God replies, *"You may not know enough but I know everything."*

As leaders we need to be encouraged that we do not have to know anything if the One who knows everything goes with us, guides us, empowers us, and protects us. With God we can do anything. By knowing God we have access to His wisdom and knowledge. Our faith in Him is a key for leading. Faith is our trust in the person of God to do what He says He will do. That includes showing us the way and empowering us to accomplish the tasks He calls us to perform.

Excuse #3: I Might Fail.

Moses is being honest with God about the way he feels. He does not want to take a responsibility and then fail. His question is one that every leader asks at some time in his experience. *"What if they will not believe me, or listen to what I say?"* (4:1). Moses wonders if he will have the ability to convince the Israelites that he has heard from God and has been appointed as their deliverance leader. It is a well-founded fear because every leader faces the same question whenever he or she begins a task. Will the people follow me? Do I really know what I'm doing? What if they refuse to listen?

I know that throughout my life I have faced these kinds of questions. It is a matter of authority, power, integrity, and mission. New leaders always face these questions as they attempt to get started in a new role. There is always the possibility of failure, but when God calls a leader He empowers that leader to succeed.

In fact, in the face of Moses' fear of failure, God gives him power that will prove his authority. In effect God is saying, *"Moses, you may fail, but I cannot."* What a blessing to anyone called and chosen by God to lead.

Excuse #4: I Have Weaknesses.

Moses is down to his last excuse now. God has responded to each of his fears and excuses and now the main fear that troubles Moses comes to light. He confesses that he is not an eloquent speaker. In fact, he states the problem specifically when he says, *"I have never been eloquent, neither recently, nor in time past, nor since Thou hast spoken to me; for I am slow of speech and slow of tongue"* (4:10). For a man unsure of himself when he speaks, Moses sure seems more than eloquent in describing his problem to God!

I like the way Eugene Peterson interprets Moses' words in *The Message*:

> *"Master, please, I don't talk well. I've never been good with words, neither before nor after you spoke to me. I stutter and stammer."* (Exodus 4:10 MSG)

Moses imagines that much of his task will be to speak to Pharaoh and to the children of Israel about the things God is doing and will do. Perhaps he projects ahead in his mind to his first meeting with Pharaoh. He is surrounded by unfriendly individuals as he stands before this great and powerful man. His words come slowly and, as his tension mounts, he begins to stutter. Soon no one can understand him. His authority is compromised and the mission fails.

God assures Moses and tells him that his brother Aaron will accompany him at every point in his task. If he cannot talk, then Aaron will be there to speak for him. In effect God is giving Moses assurance of his success by sending Aaron with him. He seems to say, *"Moses, you may have limitations and handicaps, but I do not. I am perfect, and perfectly able to deliver My people from Pharaoh."*

Can I insert another important leadership principle here? *God's call is usually to something that is beyond our background, experience, training, skill, education, and comfort level.*

Think of all the people God used in Scripture to accomplish His purposes and you will discover that He did not call and use those who had the degrees, experience, training, or skills. He used men and women who were pure in their hearts and available to Him for His purposes.

* Noah had never seen rain or a boat but he built an ark.
* Joseph had no training to manage a nation but he led Egypt.
* David was only a shepherd boy who God anointed a king.
* Isaiah felt unworthy (unclean) but God sent him as His messenger.
* Jeremiah felt too young to be a prophet but God called him.
* Nehemiah was a cupbearer who rebuilt the walls of Jerusalem.
* John the Baptist was a somewhat strange, reclusive individual who prepared the way for Christ.
* Peter was a fisherman, Matthew a tax collector, Mary Magdalene an oppressed woman, and Paul an enemy of Christ and the Church. But God used each of them to accomplish His purposes.

What you are in your relationship with God in Christ is what determines how and where God will use you. There is nothing wrong with preparation, education, experience, and training. All these things will contribute to our lives. But God calls us first to Himself and to His righteousness before He sends us to fulfill His purposes. *What you are and how you love and obey the Lord is far more important and useful to God than what you might be able to do.*

Years ago I struggled in a ministry far outside my comfort level. I am at heart a pastor and a preacher but by God's leading I served in a Christian corporation for thirteen years. In a particularly difficult time, a trusted friend told me something that I have never forgotten. *"Gene,"* he said, *"you are struggling trying to develop your skills and*

God is trying to build your character. If you will allow God to develop you into the person He wants you to be, then He will give you the skills you need to do your job."

I was stunned by the truth of what he said and I followed his advice. In fact, for the years I stayed in my position in that corporation, my greatest struggles always seemed to focus on my character and rarely ever did I sense a lack of skills for the task.

If you are struggling with the task God is calling you to, then remember that what He is looking for is a person of truth, integrity, and a willingness to trust and obey Him in everything. He will not call you to something that He will not equip you to do. Never forget that it is God who will do what He wants done. He will do it through you and with you but it is God who decrees, determines, and decides what and how something is to be done to accomplish His purposes.

Finally, I want you to know that what God calls you to is uniquely yours. We can learn from other leaders but eventually you must find your own way through your own struggles. What God calls you to is yours alone. He is raising you up right now to serve His purposes and despite your fears or doubts, you are the one He has called. It may be to stay where you are even though it's tough right now. He may move you away from what you like or feel comfortable doing. He may ask you to sacrifice something precious or valuable. He may lead you in dangerous or exciting paths. Listen to His voice and trust Him to use you in ways that honor Him and bless you.

Everyone feels the pressure of a God-sized task. The vision, the dedication, the hard work, and the risks bring us to a true assessment of who we are, what we think our capabilities are to be successful, and what threatens our completing the work. God gave Moses a huge vision, a large task, and forty years to get it accomplished. Never forget: *It takes a long time to become a great leader.* Where you begin and what you begin with is only part of the journey. How long it takes is important but that too is just another part of the whole leadership equation. How you finish and what you become over the years of your leadership life is the best and final measurement.

Chapter Two

~~~

The Leader's Work

As Moses took up the task that God gave him, his life changed immediately and enormously. It changed immediately because he left the wilderness that had been his home for the past forty years to engage the Israelites. He would also go before Pharaoh multiple times demanding his release of the Hebrews. Moses wasted no time going to his father-in-law, Jethro, asking for permission to return to his people in Egypt. Jethro gave him permission and his blessing. Moses took his wife and sons and left for Egypt. When God speaks, we obey at once.

In addition, in the short time between his burning bush experience and his return to Egypt, Moses experienced an enormous change in his life. He had been a fugitive hiding in the wilderness, shepherding sheep. From the security of the hidden places to the spotlight of Pharaoh's court, he quickly became the recognized leader of thousands of people. He vaulted into leadership and was God's spokesman to the Hebrew people and to the nation of Egypt.

Each time I read this story, I am amazed at both the change God brought to Moses' life and the short time in which that change took place. There are very few men eighty years of age who ever experience a true "meteoric" rise like Moses did. This reminds me of another key leadership principle: *A person's age does not determine what God can do through him or her.* Age is a factor but not the determining factor in what God is doing in a person's life. Moses was eighty, Aaron his brother was eighty-three, but David was only thirteen when God called him. Don't worry about your age or the "time you have left" to serve the Lord. Just get on with the work He has called you to.

As he begins to lead, Moses' learning curve is outrageously steep but there are factors that help him in his assignment. Our careful attention to what Moses experienced will serve us well as we fulfill the callings and assignments God gives us.

GOD'S POWER

That leaders need power is obvious. Without power there is no authority and without authority there is no possibility for leadership. While authority is the right to lead it is power that enables a person to lead. Secular experts on leadership grapple with the notion of power constantly. Many are convinced that the best leaders are strong in character, forceful in decision-making, and dominant in every setting. Others think that a collaborative leader is best because he invites everyone into his leadership tasks. Some favor great visionaries or perhaps good communicators. There seems to be enough diversity in organizations, churches, corporations, and nations to see how different leadership styles fit best in situations that call for differing strengths in different times.

In the end, however, if a person in authority has no power he or she cannot lead. It is impossible. A leader's communication, the power to persuade, the skills to bring change to people, and the ability to reverse declining situations depend upon authority and power. Moses knew it and God knew it when He sent him back to Egypt. God gave Moses the power to accomplish his task. But this power would reach farther than Moses imagined.

God displays His power through His servants to establish their authority in order that their words will carry weight and eventually reveal God Himself. This is the reason Moses had supernatural power.

Had he gone to the Israelites and Pharaoh with only strong words, he would have been dismissed quickly by them. But his displays of power caused the Hebrews to believe and eventually caused Pharaoh to let them go.

> *"Then Moses and Aaron went and assembled all the elders of the sons of Israel; and Aaron spoke all the words which the Lord had spoken to Moses. He then performed signs in the sight of the people. So the people believed; and when they heard that the Lord was concerned about the sons of Israel and that He had seen their affliction, then they bowed low and worshiped."* (4:29–30)

In this initial meeting Aaron spoke Moses' words and displayed Moses' power in order to show the people his integrity in his task of delivering them from their slavery. The people saw the signs, heard the words, and turned to God in worship. From this point forward, Moses will speak and do wonders, thus establishing the truth of his words and works.

There is a pattern here that is revealed clearly in the life of Christ. The Gospels show in the early ministry of Jesus that the miracles He performed established His authority to speak and the integrity of His life and mission. In one instance He exhorts a lame man to take courage because his sins are forgiven. The scribes who heard Him immediately thought He was blaspheming by acting like God who alone can forgive sins. Jesus knew their thoughts and said to them,

> *"Which is easier, to say, 'Your sins are forgiven,' or to say, 'Rise, and walk?' But in order that you may know that the Son of Man has authority on earth to forgive sins—then He said to the paralytic—'Rise, take up your bed, and go home.'"* (Matthew 9:5–8)

Matthew records that the paralytic rose and went home and the people who witnessed the miracle were *"filled with awe"* because

God had given such *authority* to men. The display of His power made His words meaningful because the power established His authority.

Moses was no different. He had no authority until he displayed the power of God in his life and through his life. A leader's power is God's power in him and displayed through him in such a way that his authority, integrity, and mission are established. In the end, however, something even more important occurs; people turn to trust and serve God in worship and honor.

The power we need in our lives is already ours. We have a gift from the Father through Jesus and it is a gift of power.

"All authority has been given to Me in heaven and on earth. Go therefore and make disciples of all the nations, baptizing them in the name of the Father, and the Son and the Holy Spirit, teaching them to observe all that I commanded you; and lo, I am with you always, even to the end of the age." (28:18–20)

What Jesus was given by the Father, He has given to us, namely, His authority to accomplish His purposes.

"And I will ask the Father, and He will give you another Helper, that He may be with you forever; that is the Spirit of Truth." (John 14:16–17)

The presence of the Holy Spirit in our lives means His power.

"And you shall receive power when the Holy Spirit has come upon you and you shall be my witnesses both in Jerusalem and in all Judea and Samaria and even to the remotest part of the earth." (Acts 1:8)

The call of God includes the power and authority of God to do what He commands. The strength and power God gives us come through our relationship with Christ. We live in Him and enjoy the strength and power of His resurrection life. Are you ready for another key leadership principle? Here it is: *God's call comes with His power and authority which He gives us to exercise.* Whatever God calls you to or whatever you are going through right now includes the power and authority to successfully complete the assignment. How long it takes or what you have to endure is something we will consider later. For now, trust God for what He has given you to serve Him.

SURROUNDED BY THE RIGHT PEOPLE

Moses had the help of a number of important people. He could not do his work without them and neither can you. It is unfortunate when leaders focus on their tasks without understanding their need of others to help them. There is no great Kingdom task that God will give a leader which will not require others. Moses was initially stunned with the assignment that God gave him. It was a large task fraught with risks and potential disaster. But Moses was not to go alone and was not to do the job alone. He had God's promise to be with him and he was initially given Aaron as a companion, support, and mouthpiece whenever he needed him.

It is easy to spend time and energy outlining visions, tasks, resources needed, potential risks, and time frames only to forget the crucial element of people. When God calls you to a task, He will give you the people you need to be successful. You might not see their value at first or even appreciate them, but in time you will. In fact, you may have to reach them, train them, and lead them before they can help you, but they will be there for you in God's will and God's time.

At first Moses had Aaron, then Jethro his father-in-law helped, and finally Joshua was at his right hand when he needed him. Each man had a different, unique, and crucial role to play in serving God by serving Moses. Eventually Moses would benefit from the skill of craftsmen who built the tabernacle, men who would help him settle

disputes among the people, and the priests who were given responsibilities for sacrifices. Do not forget that you always need people to
surround you and help you fulfill your calling. And do not get discouraged if those who will help do not have the same understanding,
passion, and gifts you do for what God is doing. They help you best
when you first help them to be their best.

You have to take this principle in faith because when you begin
your journey into a new challenge, as a leader you are often the only
one who really knows what God wants done. If you are not careful
then you will run too far ahead of your people, including those who
are going to help you. If you go too far ahead then you will only be
out for a long, lonely walk!

Pray for those God will use to help you. Spend time with them
discovering how their gifts, experience, and passion fits the purposes
God has for you and your people. Share in clear terms what God is
asking you to do and let them know how your faith is being tested
and is growing as you prepare to accomplish the task God has given.
Identify your weaknesses and look for those around you who will
strengthen you. Let them know you need their help, input, and hard
work.

I see another key leadership principle here: *You can only lead
and work with the people you have right now.* Others may come to
help you later but you need to work with those you have. Moses was
not perfect nor were the men who helped him, but together they did
staggering historical and spiritual feats which remain today as some
of the greatest events ever.

THE SPIRITUAL LEADER'S WORK

No matter what task, assignment, or mission God has given you, it
takes work. Determining how to accomplish what God has directed
is always a challenge. I have a pastor friend who confesses that he
lives in a perpetual quandary about how to do his work. He says that
when he is studying he wonders if he should be in the office doing

administrative tasks. He confesses that when he is visiting his members in the hospital he wonders if his time would be better spent with his children and his wife.

I suppose those kinds of issues will always be a part of a leader's dilemma, but there are some principles of work reflected in Moses' life that are helpful. His first days of leading the Israelites in the wilderness were not easy or effective. In fact, by the time his father-in-law Jethro came to visit him, he was in the middle of a leadership logjam. Their encounter is recorded for us in Exodus 18. Jethro brings Moses' wife and family back to him and rejoices at all Moses told him about the deliverance from Egypt.

The next day, Jethro observed Moses making judgments for the people. He did it well but he did it from morning to evening (18:13). Jethro asks Moses what he is doing and Moses replies that the people come to him inquiring of the Lord and he is making judgments in disputes among the people. Jethro's words to Moses are discerning,

> *"The thing that you are doing is not good. You will surely wear out, both yourself and these people who are with you for the task is too heavy for you; you cannot do it alone."* (Exodus 18:17–18)

We have already seen that leaders need others around them. Jethro's insight to what was happening to Moses was on target. Moses is working hard but not effectively. He is a developing leader trying his best to take care of the people's concerns and needs. It is his responsibility but not his task. It reminds me of what the Apostles told the people when some needs among the Greek widows were going unmet.

> *"It is not desirable for us to neglect the word of God in order to serve tables. But select from among you, brethren, seven men of good reputation, full of the Spirit and of wisdom, whom we may put in charge of this task. But we will devote our selves to prayer, and to the ministry of the word."* (Acts 6:2–4)

They did not say that serving tables was unimportant or that they were too good to do it. They did not push the responsibility for taking care of the widows onto others. They took responsibility for the need while keeping focused on their calling and assignments.

In a similar way, Moses was bearing the responsibility for every person and every need of every person who comprised the people of Israel. But responsibility for everything is not the same as doing everything. In my opinion, Jethro's advice is one of the great leadership discourses ever written. In general, he tells Moses to intercede for the people, to teach them what they need to know, to model what he wants them to do, and finally to multiply himself by appointing others to help him.

Specifically, he gives some great insight into how a leader is to accomplish his work. Let's look at what he said for some spiritual principles of leading that truly work.

Listener

"Now listen to me: I shall give you counsel and God be with you."

(Exodus 18:19)

Leaders talk. It is a fact that we are constantly talking about something, to someone, for many reasons. We preach and present, teach and testify, counsel and comfort, explain and encourage...well, you get the picture. But many leaders are not good listeners.

Can I confess something to you that my wife, family, and other people already know but rarely mention? I'm a terrible listener. I used to think it had something to do with my personality or my quick but wandering mind. I have the capacity to look right at you, hearing almost nothing you say as my mind wanders to faraway places. I would like to think that such multitasking is an art form but in reality it is poor leadership, not to mention rude.

Why don't we listen? It might be pride that refuses to believe anyone else can ever know as much as we know. Is it the fear that if we admit we don't know something or there is a better way to do something we might appear weak or incompetent? Is it that we have so many demands on us that we often find ourselves out of capacity to receive another problem or suggestion?

Listening begins with humility to realize that, while we have the responsibilities of leadership, we may lack skills, resources, and experience to be effective. Moses certainly had the potential to develop into a great leader but he was inexperienced and it showed as he tried to do too much.

Listening is also a skill that can be developed. Any leader can become a good listener. Good listening helps us to get crucial information, gain understanding into the issues we face, learn things we need to be effective, and in general enjoy conversation with others. Many leaders are preoccupied with other things and do not listen well. Have you ever talked to someone at a convention or meeting and instead of looking at you they look over your shoulder scanning the crowd? It makes me feel small and unimportant when it happens.

Sometimes we do not listen because we are more interested in our own opinions and views than those of the speaker. I find myself in this category too often as I hear the words someone is saying but I am either evaluating them as a person, framing a response to what is said before he or she finishes, or judging and thinking of a rebuttal I am going to offer.

Pharaoh did not listen to Moses and it cost him and his nation. The people in Noah's day refused to listen and they died. Spiritual leaders listen to wisdom and truth when it is given. They hear it, process it, and apply it.

> *"So Moses listened to his father-in-law, and did all that he had said."* (18:24)

Wow! Moses could have said to Jethro, *"Thanks for the advice, but you have never really been in this position. You are a successful man and I appreciate your opinion but I'm leading thousands of people and I don't think you quite understand."* He did not say that but acted wisely on the sound advice Jethro offered. You might be surprised what good advice someone might give you who knows little or nothing about what you do. Do not be too proud, busy, or rude to listen to the next senior adult, young person, or family member who cares enough to try to help you.

After my father retired, he went to work at Wal-Mart as a greeter. A widower, he was looking for something to do that would put him with people. He loved it and faithfully went to work each day, looking forward to seeing everyone coming into the store. He worked for ten years until his death. At his funeral, I met his store manager who told me that he and Daddy would often meet early in the morning in a quiet spot in the store. He said they would talk about work and how he could be a better manager. "Your father helped me with good advice and wisdom. I'm what I am today in large part because of the time I spent listening to him," he said.

Of course, that made my loss and grief easier to bear but it gave me a good impression of the manager. *Good leaders get better by listening to wisdom and truth from others.*

Champion

"You are the people's representative before God, and you bring the disputes to God."

(18:19)

Jethro told Moses to go before the Lord on behalf of the people. They needed him to represent them and their needs before the Lord. This advice is more poignant than may at first seem apparent. Moses was the only one at this time who had talked to the Lord. He knew Him and the plans He had for the nation, but the people had been in slavery for over four hundred years. What they knew of the Lord came from the memories of Abraham, Isaac, Jacob, and Joseph. Scripture is silent about their faith, worship, or knowledge of God. Their heritage was rich in revelation and covenant promises, but they had

MOSES ON LEADERSHIP

been away for a long time from Canaan and the promises God made to the Patriarchs.

Moses had been in constant dialogue with God. He knew Him not only as El Shaddai but also as Jehovah (Exodus 3:1). He had heard directly from God about His covenant promises made to Abraham, Isaac, and Jacob and His coming to fulfill those promises for and in the children of Israel. The people needed a spokesman, speaking for God to the people, and to God for the people.

The people would also need a mediator to intercede for their sins and needs. Someone from among the people, representing the people, needed to go before the Lord and someone from the Lord needed to go before the people. The distance between God and His people at this point was great and Moses bridged that gap.

Moses did what Jethro advised. When he went to the mountain of God to receive the Ten Commandments, the people, led by Aaron, fashioned a golden calf to worship saying, *"This is your God, O Israel, who brought you up from the land Egypt"* (32:5). Aaron followed the people's lead and built an altar for the next day's sacrifice. God told Moses to go down the mountain and view the people who had *"corrupted themselves"* by departing from the way He had commanded.

The Lord then gave this chilling judgment: *"I have seen this people, and behold, they are an obstinate people. Now then let Me alone, that My anger may burn against them, and that I may destroy them; and I will make you a great nation"* (32:9–10).

Moses' immediate response to the Lord was to plead His mercy and to ask that the people not be destroyed. He did not excuse them for their actions, but he asked on their behalf for God to spare them. His plea was based on the promises the Lord had given Abraham, Isaac, and Israel to multiply them as the stars in the heavens and to give them the Promised Land. Moses pled the promises of God for the Israelites.

> *"So the Lord changed His mind about the harm which He said He would do to His people."* (32:14)

A close look at the Israelites reveals a people often unfaithful, obstinate, unkind, rebellious, fearful, and disappointing. When the twelve spies returned from their mission and reported to Moses and the people, the Israelites grew fearful and refused to go into the land. They started a movement to return to Egypt.

> *"Then the entire congregation lifted up their voices and cried and the people wept that night....So they said to one another, 'Let us appoint a leader and return to Egypt.'"*
> (Numbers 14:1, 4)

Moses, Aaron, Joshua, and Caleb all tried to reason with the people and exhort them to trust the Lord to bring them safely into the land but they would not listen. Then the scene turned ugly.

> *"But all the congregation said to stone them with stones."* (14:10)

God declares that He has had enough of their faithlessness and complaining. He vows to destroy them but once again Moses intercedes on their behalf. He acknowledges their sins and approves God's discipline but he asks for the nation to be spared.

> *"Pardon, I pray, the iniquity of this people according to the greatness of Thy lovingkindness, just as Thou hast forgiven this people, from Egypt until now."* (14:19)

Not long ago on a trip to the Bible lands, I stood and looked over a fence separating Israel and Egypt at the area of Kadesh Barnea. It is a remote area in a wilderness. Nothing much grows there and I can imagine the Israelites' fear of their future and their comfort in their past as the spies gave their reports. But their fear turned to rebellion and the Lord had had enough of it. Yet Moses interceded. They did not deserve it, they did not ask for it, but he did it anyway. He heeded Jethro's advice.

The people you lead today may be a disappointment to you. You wish they were more faithful, respectful, and helpful. You wonder if they have any idea about what you are trying to get them to become and to do for the Lord. At every turn, you may have seen them turn away from your leadership and God's will. You look above the front door of your place each morning wondering if someone has written *"Ichabod"* above it.

You're exhausted leading them. You don't have any more ideas to motivate them or convince them of the truth. You have asked God repeatedly to let you move on and you've wondered if He has heard your pleas. I've been there and felt disappointment and rejection so severe I just wanted to lie down alone in a dark room.

Your people are not any worse than the Israelites, are they? They still need a leader who will go before God on their behalf and plead for His mercy on them. They still need a vision from God, a word from God, and a way to follow. Moses shows us that good leaders are good whether their people are or not. You do not have to pretend that things are good when they are not. But intercede for them. Pray until the Lord moves to bless them. Be the conduit to those blessings. Don't give up on them. They are God's people and you are in God's work, leading people to be and do more than they ever expected.

From Moses, we learn that *great leaders never give up on their people.* This of course is easier said than done, but leaders develop people. They get them to do what ordinarily they would not do and they lead them to become what they could never imagine becoming. God calls us to Himself and sends us to His people to equip them, serve them, protect them, and develop them into His true children.

Teacher

"Teach them the statutes and the laws."

(Exodus 18:20)

Every leader is a teacher and is responsible for teaching people in his organization. Teaching includes giving information, challenging assumptions, presenting truths that transform, and opening the doors for learning. Jethro saw Moses making judgments for the people and explaining the truths of God to them. He knew that they needed to know these laws themselves in order to live them and experience the blessings of God. But Moses could not live their lives for them. They needed instruction in the laws, statutes, and ways of God.

A leader is often the first to hear from God and to receive God's plan or vision for His people. Often it is a matter of developing that plan or vision and then communicating it to those who follow. Teaching is crucial because through teaching we communicate information, inspiration, truth, new understanding of truth, and many other things. In general, however, teaching is necessary because people do not always understand what God is doing and what He wants done. A leader spends time with the Lord and out of that time come ideas, new directions, solutions to issues being faced, and breakthroughs to new experiences.

Jethro was wise to advise Moses to teach the people God's statutes. He knew that when he did, he would deepen in his understanding of what he taught, he would affirm what God was saying, and he would establish credibility with the Israelites. If you teach something well then you have mastered your subject and your subject has mastered you. Taking time is crucial, to prepare by thinking through what you want to say and carefully crafting ways your hearers understand you. In addition, you must present your message with such clarity that no one misunderstands what you said (this is not the same as everyone accepting it) and understands how they are to receive and apply it to their lives.

My daughter is a middle school teacher. She is good at it and enjoys the students in her classes. One afternoon a former high school teacher of hers called our house asking for her. She was out and when I offered to take a message the teacher told me something about teaching I have never forgotten. He was speaking of my daughter, who had done her practice teaching under his supervision. He said there are three types of teachers. One type teaches for the money and will retire as soon as possible. The next type has mastered a subject and wants to deliver his or her discoveries of the subject. The third type, he concluded, was a person deeply interested in the students' welfare, learning, and development. Teachers in this category mastered their subject with their students in mind. He said my daughter was definitely in the third category. I remain filled with pride whenever I think about what he said about her.

Leaders are teachers and they too fall into three, similar categories. Some leaders enjoy their position and expect their people to give respect, no matter what. They are generally poor communicators and have little interest in teaching their people much of anything. A second type of leader is one who teaches his people but gives only the subject matter or information needed. This teacher's focus is on what needs to be taught. Whenever the task is complete, then it's time for another session on another subject. The best leader, however, teaches to transform his people. He knows them and their needs. He goes before the Lord on their behalf, seeking what God has for them. He then takes these truths and fashions his messages to meet their needs and change their lives.

Teaching is more than a position and more than communicating information. It is about a heart for God, for His work, and for His people. It is about developing persons according to God's truth and God's plan for His people. Leaders who teach have enormous power to change people's lives. *Great leaders teach to transform people.*

Model

Jethro continued his advice to Moses by urging him to *"make known to them the way in which they are to walk, and the work they are to do"* (18:20).

We will look at a leader's relationship with his people in another chapter. This seems like advice on how to build relationships but it is not. Jethro is outlining the work Moses is to do as he leads the Israelites to their new home. Actually he is offering a leadership task and strength that is quite old and used every day around the world. Most of our learning is intuitive in that we sense what needs to be done and how to do it. When we are shown how, we learn tasks very quickly. The Israelites not only needed to know the Lord and His laws or His will for their lives, they also needed to know how to live in a way that pleased Him.

We live in a time when most people believe that they are personally responsible for determining what they believe and how they choose to live. Scripture presents quite a different view. It clearly shows that sin has separated us from the Lord and taken away our ability to know and do what is right in God's sight. We need to be taught the way to follow God. Isaiah said it well when he wrote,

> *"'For My thoughts are not your thoughts, neither are my ways your ways', declares the Lord."* (Isaiah 55:8)

The Preacher in proverbs states it even stronger when he writes,

> *"There is a way which seems right to a man, but its end is death."* (Proverbs 14:12)

Leaders have great powers to influence people but no power is greater than what he or she models. I think of Jesus' method as the best way to teach or disciple persons and transform them into full followers of the Lord. Jesus' method was simple but effective.

* He spoke to the disciples about a subject like the Kingdom or evangelism.
* He showed them how to do what He was teaching.
* He involved them as they did a task with Him.
* He watched them or sent them out to do what He had taught them.
* He sent them out on their own to do what He commanded.

This method is probably the way your parents taught you to tie your shoes or brush your teeth. Your parents likely taught you to tie your shoelaces by first talking about it. Then you watched carefully as they tied the strings together. One day they made you pick up the strings and with their hands on yours, you tied the laces into a bow. Finally you tied your first bow with them watching to make sure the laces were tight and would stay tied. After a few times of watching, they left you to yourself and you have tied your laces perfectly ever since.

Jethro advises Moses to walk under God's statutes and show the people whatever work the people were commanded to do. In this specific case he was referring to judging the disputes the people had. Those he would appoint as judges would watch him live and judge and know exactly what to do when they judged. This would ensure consistency among the judges as well as consistency in keeping the law of God, thus pleasing Him.

Take a Moment

If you are reading this book like I read most books, you are rapidly moving through the material underlining what seems important and skimming the rest. I know you are busy but I urge you to take a moment and think about modeling God's truths, ways, and work before the people you lead. If you pastor or serve on a church staff, think about those you serve each week. If you lead an organization, consider the importance of your life to the lives of the persons under your leadership. The leader who models Christ before people has enormous power and influence.

Think about what you want for your people. Do you want to see them transformed? Do you hope to see them applying what God is showing you for them? Then evaluate your own life and your practice of these things.

Let me give you a common but negative example. I spoke to a pastor some years ago who was distressed that his church was not healthy. He spoke about the low level of spiritual life among his people, their lack of interest in others, and the absence of evangelism in the church. He admitted that they were generous in giving to missions and helping members with needs but did not reach out to others effectively.

He asked if I would come and preach one weekend and I agreed. I arrived on Friday and spoke to some men who met regularly for fellowship and inspiration. On Saturday, I met with some church leaders for lunch and that night we dined with more leaders. Sunday morning, I preached for him and Sunday evening we enjoyed a church fellowship following the evening service. At the end of the weekend, I concluded that he was right in his assessment of his church. They were not particularly friendly and they talked mostly about their busy lives. No mention was made of evangelism, discipleship, or ministry throughout the weekend by anyone.

What surprised me most, however, was that the pastor never mentioned these things either. He hardly spoke to his people. When we were eating out, there were several uncomfortable silences. It was obvious that he did not know the people, even though he had been there for nearly six years. I asked him about his devotional life and study habits, including what he was reading and what God was revealing to him. He confessed that he did not have private devotions and he stressed that he was too busy to read much. He actually bristled when I asked if he had witnessed to anyone or led anyone to faith in Christ lately. You get the picture, right? Another key leadership principle pops up here. *You cannot lead people where you have not gone or are unwilling to go.* In short, if you don't, they won't! Your people will not witness if you do not. They will not be friendly if you are not friendly. You cannot change or challenge them to do things you refuse to do.

I have another confession to make. I am a certified introvert. Now many people who know me simply don't believe me when I say this but it is true. I was born with an innate shyness which makes going into new situations and meeting new people almost unbearable. I'm the guy at the restaurant who will sit alone in a far corner with a book or magazine and be completely content.

I'm not this way around people in my family or friends I know and trust, but strangers are a challenge for me. However, I have learned that although my personality may be a bit different, I do not have to actually *act* shy or retiring around people. In fact, over the years I have simply overruled my introversion and become friendly. I really do like people so one day I decided to show it. I enjoy personal evangelism so I share my faith as often as I can, despite any personal reluctance I may have.

Most importantly, however, I know that the way I live confirms what I say and what I preach to my people. I, like you, have my battles with sin, Satan, and the flesh, but I know that my life is as powerful an influence as my words.

The best way to get someone to do something is to convince them it is important, show them how to do it, help them learn to do it, and to free them up to do it.

Examine your life honestly to see if there are areas that you are not consistently modeling to your spouse, children, and other people. Change what you have to and with God's help start helping people to change their own lives.

Overseer

Jethro's final advice to Moses was to choose the right people to help him, organize them, free them to do their work, and oversee their progress. A leader's work is simply to take a big idea, such as a strategic vision, and transform it into reality. This can only be done through others unless the enterprise, organization, or entity is so small that one person *can* do it alone.

Moses led thousands of persons, with millions of needs, for forty years in a wilderness where food was only available daily and water only when they really needed it. His daily to-do list must have been impressive: people to feed, decisions on directions to march today, security threats, tabernacle construction, teaching, meeting with the Lord, judging disputes, family time, time for writing down all the laws God was giving, and who knows what else? He had to work with his people to work through them to accomplish their tasks.

Let's look at Jethro's suggestions to Moses on how to oversee the work of the judges.

CHOOSE THE RIGHT PEOPLE

The most critical decision you make as a leader is choosing the right persons to help you and your church or organization. Since most of our problems are people problems, we leaders need to carefully choose those who help us. We often feel the pressure of time or lack of resources and we put people into places where they are likely to fail. When they fail then we fail and God's work is hindered. People need to be matched with their tasks and expectations or they will end up discouraged, frustrated, or even angry.

Notice the qualifications Jethro outlined for Moses' helpers.

"Furthermore, you shall select out of all the people able men who fear God, men of truth, those who hate dishonest gain." (Exodus 18:21)

These were to be skilled (able) men who feared God, told and lived the truth, and could not be bought as judges. Remember this list is for those who would help Moses make judgments over the people's disputes. We see similar lists for servants in Acts 6 and for pastors and deacons in the early church, 1 Timothy 3, and Titus 1. The lists are heavy on moral and spiritual strengths. Another leadership principle we learn from Moses is to *choose those who help you wisely. If you have to choose between character and skill, choose character.* A lack of skills can be overcome in an organization or church easier than a lack of character. In fact, skills can be taught faster than character can develop.

You do not have to choose between skills and character, however. They are both important and both can reside in people at the same time. No one you lead has all the skills they will ever need to serve the Lord and no one is perfect. So, like Moses, your focus on the people you lead must include building skills and character simultaneously.

ALIGNMENT

Jethro told Moses to organize his helpers in manageable groups with ascending responsibility and authority beginning with the smallest to the largest group. Moses appointed judges over groups of tens, fifties, hundreds, and thousands. He was the ultimate or chief judge but these men were responsible for judging to the best of their ability over their groups.

I do not believe that you can organize for success unless you have the right conditions. Organizational alignment is crucial for success but without the right vision (that is, the big idea), strategies, resources, people, and work processes, organizations will struggle and ultimately fail. Alignment takes into consideration the people you have to work with, the work they have to do, the forces they face that hinder or help them, and the culture in which they work.

Leaders are responsible for organizational alignment that allows the will of God to be achieved. Everything important demands some organization which in turn calls for the proper alignment of people, work, and resources. We want the maximum output with the least effort in the shortest amount of time possible. Moses did this in his organization by finding able persons with impeccable character to be judges.

Many times the alignment of persons conforms to the skills of those we lead. The best people need to lead and serve in responsible positions. Some need to lead under close supervision and others need less watching over. This is true in Sunday School and small-group organizations or major corporations. It is your responsibility to align your people for successfully doing God's will and accomplishing God's purposes.

LET THEM WORK

Jethro's final word to Moses was to let the men he chose do their jobs.

"Let them judge the people at all times; and let it be that every major dispute they will bring to you, but every minor dispute they themselves will judge." (18:22)

There are work tasks that a leader cannot give away such as communicating, envisioning, strategy, financial management, policy development and enforcement, etc. But much of an organization's work is done by people enlisted, hired, or secured to fulfill those roles. If the right people are chosen and they are aligned properly for their work, then they can do what needs to be done.

God has not called you and me to lead our churches and/or organizations without providing us with the persons who can help us. Moses had Jethro, Aaron, Joshua, and many others to help him. Most of those who helped him were slaves in Egypt, not captains of armies, priests, or judges. But God raised them up just like He raised Moses, to fulfill important roles. When the Israelites entered the Promised Land, their roles changed again. But remember, whatever God has called you to do, He will provide what you need to do it.

You may feel like you do not have enough people to be an effective church or organization right now. You think about the people you have to work with and you don't see how much is going to get done. What you need to do is reexamine your assignment from the Lord and see how it fits right now with the people you have. You may have to spend time building leadership or taking time to carefully model what you want them to do. You may have to communicate more of God's vision for them until they begin to see it clearly. You may have to disciple and mentor some men and women for the roles you need filled.

Church growth, health, and development, just like any organization, are constant processes. In addition, they are long processes. Moses spent forty years preparing the people to inhabit their new home, as a nation and not as a collection of slaves. They had to know the Lord, to follow His ways, and to keep His laws. Moses had to find out who was with him and who was not. He had to develop leadership that would provide for the people and protect them. He had to mentor Joshua and prepare him to take over leadership when Moses was no longer around.

You and I have to do the same thing. How you do it and how long it takes is different for each leader, but we must do it. I learned long ago that the only church I can pastor is the one I currently pastor and the only people I can lead are the ones I have right now. I may anticipate different needs requiring different leadership in the future, but right now I have to lead the people God has given me.

* I have to teach them what God is teaching me.
* I have to show them how this works in my daily life.
* I have to show them how to do their work.
* I have to put them in the right organization.
* I have to let them do their assigned work.

A leader has to have great faith in God in order to trust His people. Remember that your work is God's work and your people are God's people. He has entrusted to us all the Kingdom work on Earth. Through local churches and with the help of Christian organizations, we are to fulfill the Great Commission and prepare this world for the coming of Christ. He will build our churches if we trust Him and follow His leading.

The great benefit of leading God's way is that we are blessed to see the people we lead develop into the men and women who please Him by walking in His ways and doing His will. In addition, we enjoy leading for a long time without wearing our people out or burning out ourselves.

Jethro promised Moses that if he followed his advice they would bear most of the burdens of judging the people and he would *endure and all these people also will go to their place in peace"* (18:23).

When you lead God's way, you can do it for a long time and over a long time you will develop into an even greater leader. Moses gives us another leadership principle here, namely that *whatever God has called you to do you can do with the people you have.* It takes faith, time, and hard work, but you can do it.

It takes a long time to become adept at leading persons and developing them into highly skilled, mature believers. Every leader must learn to develop persons, put them in the places God wants for them, and help them successfully do the work He assigns.

Nearly every leader is good at establishing a vision and building enthusiasm in his people. Normally, leaders communicate well, have a high level of leadership skills, and possess good character. Few, it seems, have the experience to develop persons through transforming experiences that develop their lives as they serve the Lord. *It takes time to become a great leader.*

Chapter Three

≈∽∽≈

The Leader's Core

I thought a long time before coming up with a title for this important chapter. The word *core* can mean many things but to me it means the very center and soul of a leader. The part of a leader that grounds him in everything he is and everything he does. It is the center of his decision making, his conduct, and his morals. It is what truly defines a leader because skills may enable a leader to function, but his character will enable him to know the right thing and do it whatever it costs. Plus, how can a leader develop character in others if it is not developed in himself?

We live in a day where biblical truths for Christian leaders are being set aside for cultural mores. For instance, I think David Wells has correctly identified this problem when he writes that our culture is making dangerous substitutions for biblical realities. He says (quoted in *Baptist Press*, July 16, 2007) that we are:

* Shifting our focus from pursuing virtues to values.
* Talking less about character while promoting outward personality.

* Moving from thinking about universal human nature to exalting the individual self.
* Moving our attention away from guilt to shame.

Christian leaders face the constant dangers of ignoring the culture or succumbing to the culture. What makes a leader strong, courageous, relevant, and effective is his relationship with God. What God reveals to a leader will transcend age, culture, fads, and any of the latest ideas. We have already seen from Moses' life that God was delivering the Israelites from Egypt and He was leading them in the wilderness. It was God who gave the land to His children and it was God who prepared the land for their occupation.

God gives to His leaders what they need in wisdom, discernment, vision, resources, opportunities, and protection. What He cannot force on a leader is character. Every leader has skills but, as many of us have learned as a true principle of leadership, *your skills may take you where your character cannot keep you.*

I have stopped counting the number of leaders who in my lifetime have failed morally and spiritually despite having incredible gifts for ministry. These individuals had charisma, abilities, and opportunities that most of us will never have but they are no longer in ministry because they either lacked character or their spiritual growth stopped.

Moses was a man whose leadership developed as his character developed. He was not a perfect man by any means. He murdered an Egyptian and his anger later cost him the opportunity to enter the Promised Land. But despite his faults, he spent time with God and his leadership centered in his character not his skills.

Without a doubt all he received from God influenced him. The laws, statutes, and face-to-face meetings he had with the Lord changed his life and made him a better man and a better leader. Whenever I read the accounts of his life in Exodus, Leviticus, Numbers, and Deuteronomy, I see him change from an impulsive, fearful man wandering around shepherding sheep to a man who could face Pharaoh with strength and conviction. I see a man whose character developed into an humble leader filled with the truth, strength, and wisdom of God.

I think Deuteronomy 34:7 speaks well of Moses when it says,

"Although Moses was one hundred and twenty years old when he died his eye was not dim, nor his vigor abated."

The writer goes on to conclude that no prophet since Moses has been like him. He knew the Lord face-to-face, he performed signs and wonders that could not be matched, and God gave him great, terrifying power that astounded Israel and overcame Pharaoh. His power came from his relationship with the Lord and the consistency of his life, putting into practice what God taught him.

If you are going to be a great leader then your core must be strong; so strong that nothing can defeat you. You have to withstand satanic attack, cultural ridicule, unfaithful persons, temptations, seasons of sins, resistance to change, and sometimes rejection. You may suffer for doing God's will. You may lose your way at times and have to refocus or regroup. A leader's life is not easy. If your God is not able to form your character then you will not last.

God calls leaders to Himself to serve His purposes. The call of God on your life was His decision. You are a leader, period. But the decision about what kind of leader you will be is yours. Will you be a good one or a poor one? Will you faint in doing the work of the Lord when the times are severe or will you persevere and finish your course?

No one can exempt God's leaders from hardships, struggles, and conflicts. But the determining factor in whether you fail or not *is* your decision—a decision to seek the Lord, learn from Him and live out what He says. If you live and serve the Lord long enough, it is likely you will be hurt, criticized, and maybe dismissed. Those things are outside factors that only a strong character can help you withstand.

A friend of mine called me one Monday morning to ask if he might come by my office. We met that day and he told me he had been dismissed from his church the previous day. He told of the conflict that led to the action of the church. He honestly admitted mistakes he made and how he could have perhaps done better in some areas.

He was also honest in his convictions about what his church had done. He did not agree with the accusations and actions of church members and he clearly stated why he felt they were improper. He gave an honest account of how he felt about what had happened and as I listened I noticed there was no fear, bitterness, or rancor in his voice. He expressed his disappointment without blaming others. I could only conclude that this pastor had character, a core within his life that was keeping him strong and steady. I marveled to listen to him speak about his next steps and his confidence in the future.

He asked for any help I could give him and I readily agreed to do so. I asked him to list for me what he considered his strengths and he outlined them without hesitation. Once again, I noticed that he spoke of his gifts and desires without any pride or overestimation. He knew who he was; he had faith that God would protect him and his family from harm. He was saddened by what had happened but he was ready for his next assignment. When he left that day I felt honored that we met together because I had learned so much. *Godly character cannot be defeated.*

The foundation for Moses' and the Israelites' character were the Ten Commandments in Exodus 20. These ten declarations have proven the test of time and continue to influence millions of persons throughout the world. Throughout history, nations have used the Ten Commandments as the foundations for laws and legal codes. Ethical constructs, social behaviors, and cultural practices have been influenced by the Commandments. They reveal God's character and move us to take up His character in our relationships with others. They are spiritual gold for leaders. Jesus said that He came to fulfill the law and in doing so opened up the possibility that our lives might reflect His life.

Although we live in a different era from Moses, we can learn how biblical revelation serves as the foundation for our character. Your leadership core must be shaped from something or somewhere. A Christian leader's core is shaped by God's Word and truth. It is a standard that demands our best and complete devotion. Without God's truth we cannot have God's character. Without God's character we cannot do God's will and fulfill His purposes for our lives.

The Ten Commandments reveal the value God puts on our relationships. We will talk more about our relationships with our people in a later chapter, but we must see that character is key to leading others.

BUILDING YOUR CORE

The Commandments divide naturally into two sections. The first speaks to our relationship with the Lord and the second to our relationships with others. Each one builds upon the others and each one has a specific way to build character.

1. God Must Be First: "You shall have no other God before Me."

It is not hard to understand the meaning of the first commandment but it is a challenge to follow it completely. Is there anything in your life that you could not live without right now? How about your spouse or children? Could you live without your position or income? Could you ever see yourself living a lesser lifestyle or losing your home?

Our greatest concerns become our gods whether we know it or not. To put God first is to deny ourselves everything before we surrender our lives to the Lord. I have not noticed God ruining leader's lives but I have noticed leaders ruining their own lives by slowly putting God behind things like their ambitions, families, security, and fame. Most of the time these things don't take us over like a tsunami but rather like a slow leak into our lives.

Over time, things become more important than God. Jesus called those things *mammon* and He taught that we would become slaves to them and would eventually hate God. Many things can rule our lives and destroy us. But we can and must decide daily that God is first in

everything, every time, in every circumstance. I testify to you that I
have learned this truth from some of the hardest lessons possible. I
know in my head this is true but my heart has deceived me in the past
and my leadership has paid a terrible price for it.

A Lesson from a Broken Man

I preached one evening in a church I served as a young staff member
and one of our deacons came forward saying that he had given the
Lord all of his life that night. Although I do not remember much
about the sermon, I can never forget what happened later. My wife
and I had just gone to bed when the phone rang and the man who had
come forward in the service was crying.

He told about leaving church that night and getting caught in
a strong rain storm. He pulled under a bridge to wait for the rain to
slacken when God began to speak to him. The conversation he re-
called went something like this:

"John," the Lord said, "You've given Me your whole life tonight
have you?"

"Yes, Lord," John replied. "I give you everything."

"John, I'm going to take your wife tonight. In your grief people
will see how much I mean to you and I will use it to bring others to
Christ."

"Oh, Lord, no, don't do that. I cannot live without my wife," John
begged.

"Then, I will take your grandson, whom you love so much," God
said.

"No, Lord, not my precious grandson. He is so young and means
so much to us," John explained.

"All right, John," God went on, "I'll take your business. Your loss
will prove to others that you love Me more than your work."

"Not my business, Lord," John said, now in a panic. "I've worked
twenty-five years to build that business and provide for my family and
give to your work."

"John, I am going to take your health away and in your suffering I will show people how much you love me," God replied.

"Please, God, not my health. If I get sick no one will take care of everyone I'm responsible for in my family," John pleaded.

John then told me something that I will never forget. He said God finally said,

"John, tell Me again—what exactly did you give Me tonight? What did you mean by everything?", the Lord asked.

Jesus said it clearly in Matthew:

"He who loves father or mother more than Me is not worthy of Me; and he who loves son or daughter more than Me is not worthy of Me. And he who does not take up his cross and follow after me is not worthy of Me. He who has found his life shall lose it, and he who has lost his life for my sake shall find it. (Matthew 10:37–38)

You will not have to worry about your core if God is always first.

2. God Only: "You shall not make for yourself an idol…or worship or serve them."

After thoughtful reflection, I have concluded that I have never seen a Christian or Christian leader fashion an idol representing the Lord. I have been around the world and have viewed many idols that persons worship, but not Christians. We may have artwork depicting Jesus the man or saints who are remembered but no statues, pictures, or sculptures of the Lord God Jehovah. It just isn't done.

What I have seen and heard, however, are many depictions of what God is like and what He wills that I did not think came from Him. Idolatry is the same whether we do it with our hands or our minds. It always is a matter of the heart and the heart is the seat of character. What can be known of God is known through revelation, intuitively, in nature, through His Word, and in Jesus Christ. We remember the words of Paul to the Romans when he wrote,

> *"That which is known about God is evident <u>within them</u>; for God made it evident to them. For since the creation of the world His invisible attributes, His eternal power and divine nature, have been <u>clearly seen through what has been made</u>."* (Romans 1:19–20)

And in Hebrews we read:

> *"God after He spoke long ago to the fathers in the prophets in many portions and in many ways, in these last days has spoken to us in His Son."* (1:1–2)

The greatest danger I can think of is to claim to be a Christian and actually worship a god who does not exist. God is not who we think He is or who we want Him to be. He is far beyond what we could ever imagine. He must reveal Himself, His ways, and His will to us or we will never know them.

One danger leaders face is to represent God in ways that do not reveal Him, His character, or His purposes. To speak for God or to speak of God without true knowledge of Him is the same as idolatry. To lead people to reach our own dreams and not God's vision is dangerous, sinful, and ends in failure. We have to be mindful that people expect us to be truthful whenever we ask them to give, go, and do something in God's name. Preachers must speak God's Word, teachers must teach God's Word, and leaders must know God's will for His people. There is no excuse for a lack of study, preparation, or time in prayer. Failure to hear from God is to depend upon ourselves, believing and acting as if we know more than God about what needs to be communicated, taught, or done.

Leaders live near a dangerous path which leads to idolatry if we do not watch our lives. We are busy, pressed for time, always trying to get things done. It is easy to understand how our work can rob us of time for seeking God, studying the Bible, praying, and preparing to speak. No one sees us do these important things. People notice if we make the meetings, appointments, and visits but not if we spend time hearing from God.

I have been guilty of inserting my opinions and my will into the lives of persons I lead. It is not only unpleasant but in the end a waste of time. You and I have been called to God and then given assignments to fulfill. The Kingdom of God does not rest on our expertise, experience, thoughts, dreams, and plans. It is Christ's Kingdom to reign over and build. It is Christ's Church to build and protect. Our people are His. He saved them and He uses them for His glory. We are stewards of everything we touch in our work—stewards of the messages we give, the work we do and assign, the churches we serve, and the organizations we run.

Taking our cues from Moses we learn that great leadership happens when *leaders do what God wants, teach what we have learned from Him, go where He sends, and never initiate anything on our own without His permission.*

Failure to follow these principles is a lack of character and will eventually land us in failure.

3. In God's Name: "You shall not take the name of the Lord your God in vain."

A simple definition of vanity is *empty*. That is, anything that is vain has no substance. It is nothing, can do nothing, and ultimately has no value. My parents taught me to obey this commandment by never using the Lord's name in a curse or as a curse word. The Lord's name was the one name that we were to give ultimate respect.

I often think about what I learned from my parents and what I hear said today. People use the word "god" to show surprise, anger, or pleasure. "Oh my g—!" and "dear g—!" are common expressions, even among believers. Certainly these are examples of what the commandments teach.

But I think it is much more than that. Taking God's name in vain is using His name in any manner which would ultimately not reveal Him, glorify Him, or His purposes. Leaders create many activities, programs, worship services, ministries, and mission trips. We do so with every intention of serving the Lord. How many times, however, do we stop and consider whether what we intend to do will actually promote His name? What we do may put a favorable light upon us or our church but what glory does God get from it?

If we do as the Lord directs then we will have favor with men and with Him. But if we mimic things in culture and call them spiritual, then we are taking God's name in vain. I truly believe the Lord gives us great freedom in the ways we serve Him. We have freedom in organizing our churches, styles of worship, programs, buildings, and days and times for worship. But with that freedom must come the understanding of our responsibility to make the name of our God and His Son Jesus known among the nations.

I want my leadership to create an atmosphere where God is present, known, worshiped, and served. I want our church to be known as a place where God is worshiped, loved, followed, and respected. If no one ever knows my name or praises us for our ministries but knows God is our God and Jesus His Son is our Lord, then I can be happy.

Like all the Commandments, this one is easy to break without realizing it. The words we use, the things we do, and the initiatives we create as leaders must pass through a filter that asks if this is in vain. If God is not honored or, worse, if He is hidden or made small, we must not do it.

4. Rest and Refocus: "Remember the Sabbath day to keep it holy."

In my childhood, Sunday was a day when two things happened: worship and nothing else! We attended church in the morning and again at night. We ate a quick lunch, took naps, read, and watched sports on television but there was no work done. The pace was slow and easy, which allowed my father and mother to recover from their week of hard work. My sister and I did not work except to clean the lunch dishes. We never did homework, yard work, or housework. We rested.

I have come to understand the value of resting and refocusing on at least one day of the week. When I held a corporate position, the weekend for me was a time to get away from the pressure at work. When I was starting a new ministry, I found it easy to give all my time and energy to get things going. Now as a pastor I find I need a day away from duties in order to stay fresh, avoid discouragement, and lead effectively.

Leaders are by nature aggressive, hard-charging folks. We like to get things done quickly in order to be successful and enjoy the fruits of our labors. We think about our jobs a lot and spend all the time possible working while trying to balance our marriages, families, and other interests we may have. But God knows best and He has decreed that we rest.

God designed a day of rest, worship, and refocus in order that we might meet the demands of the other days successfully. To observe a day of rest and worship is to focus on God and not on ourselves. God allows us to work on our lives through the week but one day is for our minds, souls, and bodies to recover and our hearts to seek Him. No one can work effectively very long without rest. Something will break down in us physically, mentally, spiritually, or in some combination.

It is a sin not to rest and refocus because it violates one of the commands God gave to help us live and work. Every leader needs to determine what it means to rest and how best to do it. We rarely think of the value of rest as it relates to building character but it is valuable. When a leader experiences burnout, a nervous breakdown, a moral failure, or heart attack, we rush to help. It takes months or years to overcome these conditions which could have been avoided by following God's command to rest and refocus.

When I am fatigued for an extended period, I am a target for the Enemy to tempt me to a moral or spiritual failure. I am more easily discouraged, weary in well doing, and willing to quit. The pressures we deal with as leaders demand that we have rest and diversion. Character is impossible to develop when we are flirting with sin and temptation or depressed and tired.

5. Honor Your Family: "Honor your father and mother."

This may seem a strange commandment to apply to the core character of a leader but it is important. I had the fortune to grow up in a good, solid family. My father was a man of faith and outstanding character. My mother loved my sister and me and taught us well. We had little family conflict, plenty to eat, a good place to live, nice clothes to wear, and enough money to spend. No one was perfect in our household but we lived well and loved one another.

You may not have been blessed with the kind of life that I had growing up. Your parents may not have provided well or they may even have divorced. You may have endured abuse, alcoholism, or even abandonment. You may have grown up with little or no love for your father or mother. How you were treated may not have been your fault and your experience may have been hard.

I do not think it is unreasonable for anyone to honestly assess his family for what it truly was. If your father was not a loving, providing, or protecting man, you should not try to make him into something he wasn't. If your mother never nurtured you or showed you love that you needed, there is no reason to make up something.

Giving honor to a parent is something we choose to do, something that really has nothing to do with how they treated us. Character is built by doing the right thing because God says it is the right thing. When we give honor and respect to our parents, we give honor to God. He gave us life through our parents. They may have chosen things that did not help us, but our honor to them is not based on how we were treated but how God wants us to treat them.

If you are fortunate to have living parents, then honor them with your words and actions in a way that reflects your relationship with your Heavenly Father. You might not be able to see them but you can honor them in the way you speak of them. Once again, you should not pretend that who they were and what they did (or did not do) was good. You can thank God He used them to bring you to life on Earth. You can thank Him for the good things they did and for how you turned out despite their faults. You can do so with a heart to honor God.

I cannot honor my parents tangibly because they are deceased. I can, however, honor their memories by speaking of them with favor. I have told my children and grandchildren about them with stories that make us laugh, cry, and be thankful.

An important thing to remember is this: *"The way a leader speaks about people, especially his parents, reveals much about his character."*

6. Treat Life as Precious: "You shall not murder."

Historically Christians have treated all of life as precious. In the sundry laws the Lord gave to Moses, it is apparent that human life is more valuable than possessions. In Israel a person who stole something was required to make restitution but no harm to that person was allowed. If a person harmed another, the principle of an eye for an eye and a tooth for a tooth limited retribution in order to protect life. If a person murdered someone, he had committed a crime so extreme that he had to surrender his own life.

I have sometimes wondered what Moses thought when God gave him this commandment. His memory of his murder of the Egyptian must have caused him to freeze before the Lord. His impulsive act changed his life forever as he fled to the wilderness. Instead of enjoying the benefits of Pharaoh's court, his life was reduced to tending the flocks of his father-in-law.

God is the creator of life and we are to uphold life with a passion. As leaders, we might wonder how this commandment helps to shape our character. I'm sure most of us have not committed murder, so what could be the issue? Jesus gives us some help in His teaching in Matthew.

"You have heard that the ancients were told, 'you shall not commit murder and whoever commits murder shall be liable to the court.' But I say unto you that everyone who is angry with his brother shall be guilty before the court; and whoever shall say to his brother, 'Raca,' shall be guilty before the supreme court, and whoever shall say, 'You fool,' shall be guilty enough to go into the fiery hell." (Matthew 5:21–23)

Does it amaze you that the Lord puts murder, anger, and name-calling like "empty head" (i.e., *good for nothing*) and *fool* in the same category? I understand that murder is an awful sin, but anger and careless words? What surfaces is that God holds all life as significant, precious, and valuable, and nothing is to be done or said that will not support this value.

Leaders who treat people with contempt reveal characters that God will not use. Anyone who tears a person apart with destructive words is not in God's will and will not honor Him. Every leader constantly evaluates persons and deals with difficult people. We often find ourselves in conflict with people we serve and people who work for us. But our tongues reflect whether we value people or not.

Words like "fool," "dummy," and "idiot" reveal how the speaker truly feels about someone. When we use such terms, whether in public or in private, we sin against God and the person we are talking about. Right now, I would really like to move to the next commandment because I'm feeling a spiritual *ouch* that I had not planned on feeling. How about you? I know few pastors and Christian leaders who do not violate this commandment.

It is our responsibility as Kingdom stewards to see people like the Lord sees them. We need to remember that He creates them and seeks to save them from their sins. We need to remember that believers often act like fools and persons without sense. When they do, we do not need to label them. We have to be honest about their behavior but they do not need our condemning judgments.

I imagine that there are more ways to sin with the tongue than any other part of the body. And the tongue is only an extension of the mind and heart. If you say it, you mean it, and if you say something God forbids about another person, then you reveal your lack of character.

Leaders need a solid core of character that causes them to refrain from judging persons and instead to honestly evaluate them while doing everything possible to develop their lives.

A leader who honors God by honoring others can make difficult decisions about people. He can lead a church or organization successfully while displaying grace even in conflict. A godly leader deals fairly and firmly with people who do not perform or who live sinfully. He holds people accountable for their lives, commitments, and responsibilities without stooping to caustic judgments about the people he leads. He is neither too soft nor too hard on people. He is spiritual and Christlike.

Moses dealt with thousands of difficult people. He faced their criticism, sins, unfaithfulness, murmuring, and rebellion. He was honest about who they were and what they did without judging them with condemning words.

Honor your people and build them up despite their faults. My father used to tell me when I would be critical of others, "Son, everyone has a story and we don't always know why people do what they do." He was right, of course, and I never saw him label persons who said and did things he would never approve. Use your words wisely to help your people. Moses teaches us that, *every person is created by God, in His image, for His purposes. We have to watch what we say about them. He loves them and sent His Son to redeem them.*

7. Be Faithful to Your Spouse: "Do not commit adultery."

We live in a sexual society. Sex is a common offering in television commercials, in movies, on the web, and in print. No leader alive today is exempt from dealing with sexual temptation because it is pervasive. An immoral leader forfeits his or her right to lead because immorality reveals a flawed, sinful character. Adultery breaks a bond that God has joined between a man and a woman which He never intends to be broken.

I have been in ministry for over forty years and the number of pastors and Christian leaders who have ruined their lives or had their lives ruined because of adultery is staggering to me. The most successful leader is one who learns to love and live in a lifetime relationship with his spouse. It is God we serve and not ourselves. No one can look into the future and predict how life will change in marriage for a husband and wife. Everyone changes, but those changes do not have to make us selfish or immoral. Faithfulness to a spouse is faithfulness to the Lord.

When God gave Moses this command it must have been startling. Although some persons (even leaders) in the Bible had multiple wives, either through divorce or bigamy, God's plan is one man and one woman married until death. Faithfulness in marriage reflects God's faithfulness to His people throughout history. His covenant with Abraham was unchangeable despite Israel's unfaithfulness and rebellion. He did not change nor did His love cease as Israel sinned against Him.

My mind drifts again to Jesus' teaching in the Sermon on the Mount on this subject.

"You have heard that it was said, 'you shall not commit adultery,' but I say to you, that everyone who looks on a woman to lust for her has committed adultery with her already in his heart." (Matthew 5:27–28)

Ouch! There is another dimension of faithfulness that I would rather be excused from if it were possible. God speaks to every leader to say that your actions may be proper while your mind is unfaithful. When that happens, your life, leadership, and marriage are at risk. To harbor impure thoughts opens the door for the Enemy to bring ruin to you. The price of unfaithfulness a leader pays is exorbitant. You can lose your spouse, break apart your family, and surrender your ministry. Your call remains but your lack of character reduces your effectiveness and may eliminate you from ministry.

Years ago a friend of mine committed adultery and had to leave his church. He was a high-profile minister and his sin was well known. His church suffered for years afterward. His wife stayed with him but struggled to understand why it happened. His children were so affected they required years of counseling. I would talk to him frequently to let him know that I was praying for him and would support him in any way I could.

We talked for years without actually speaking of the one-time event that caused so much pain in his life. One day he said, "Gene, you have to believe me, it was only one time, just once." I did believe him but I asked him to tell me something that I think he had avoided for years. I asked him about what he had looked at and thought about before anything happened. He shamefully admitted that he had filled his mind with improper things and would often think about being with women who were not his wife.

Purity is gained and lost long before opportunities for immorality come. Determine now that you will never yield your mind to anything improper and that you will honor God by being faithful to your spouse for as long as either of you live. God let Moses know that *great leaders remain faithful to their spouses in all areas of their lives.*

The present age presents numerous sexual temptations that will ruin any leader. God permits sex between a married man and woman and no one else. Every other sexual act is immorality, which cannot honor God nor fulfill His will for us. Paul exhorted Timothy to flee from his lusts before he acted on them. Sexual immorality begins with a corrupted mind before physical acts transpire. *Great leaders are and remain sexually pure.*

8. Do Not Steal: "You shall not steal."

God's law is based on His ownership of all things. In Exodus 19:6 the Lord declares that *"all the earth is Mine."* The Psalmist declares, *"The earth is the Lord's, and all it contains, the world, and those who dwell in it."* In reality, God owns everything, so to steal from anyone is to steal from God. Integrity is a key, core ingredient in the character of a leader. No leader can put up with stealing and no great leader steals. He will not steal time by not working hard, he will not steal a pen from the church office, nor will he pad an expense account.

Stealing shows a lack of trust in God to provide for our needs. It may reveal a lack of financial control. Paul warns Timothy not to appoint men for pastoral leadership who are not free from the love of money. I have worked with many leaders serving churches and in Christian organizations who did not manage their money well. Financial difficulties may plague every leader at times but these seasons are not reasons to steal. Misuse of church credit cards, taking cash from the office, not paying for coffee and snacks, and printing personal documents without paying for them is stealing.

Paul writes to the Corinthians that in regard to the offering he was taking for the Jerusalem church, he took every precaution not to be discredited or charged with mishandling of the funds collected. He goes on to write, *"For we have regard for what is honorable, not only in the sight of the Lord, but also in the sight of men"* (2 Corinthians 8:21). That is a good rule for leaders to follow when dealing with finances, both personal and church or organizational.

Taking anything that is not yours destroys your character and limits your effectiveness as a leader. Your integrity must never be compromised in any area of your life and work.

9. Don't Lie: "You shall not bear false witness."

Most people agree that lying is not a good thing but what they generally mean is being lied to or lied about. Lying is so pervasive in our culture that we almost expect people to lie whenever it suits their advantage. People lie about their achievements, their faults, their actions, and anything else that will keep them out of trouble for the moment.

Think about common lies that leaders offer:

* "I had no knowledge of that."
* "I didn't do it."

* "I'll take care of it."
* "I appreciate your feedback."
* "Don't worry; everything is fine. You are okay."

I heard only recently about a church staff member who was told by his new pastor that he was going to be part of the team and not to worry. The next Sunday the pastor introduced the man's replacement to the congregation—in front of the stunned staff member!

A lie destroys any fabric of a relationship between a leader and persons who follow him. If you lie, then you cannot lead. You may manage to get your way or push people to accomplish what you want, but you will never lead. The heart of a great leader is integrity that is built on honesty.

In fact, honesty is the foundation for most of the laws and commandments that Moses received from the Lord. Jesus claimed to be the way, the truth, and the life. He prayed to the Father in John 17 that His followers would be sanctified in the truth that He had given them in God's Word. We are exhorted to love the truth, live the truth, speak the truth, and not lie to anyone. An honest person will avoid many temptations to sin that might destroy him.

When I worked in a corporation, the temptation to lie came often. It is hard to look people in their eyes and tell them bad news about working conditions or whether they are going to lose their jobs. It is tempting to fudge performance numbers when they are not good. It was tempting to promise things to critics that would quiet their criticisms, knowing that such promises would never be fulfilled.

I remember with clarity a situation when I led a division in a corporation when we implemented a new corporate software system. It paralyzed our customer service center for weeks. Our employees were stretched to their limits, working long hours handling frustrated customers who could not place orders or did not get correct orders. One Saturday I went with one of my leaders to meet with the managers in that area. I had to confront a group of tired, weary, and hopeful men and women with bad news. I wanted to say that things were going to improve quickly but that wasn't going to happen. It was one of the hardest things I ever had to do. In the end, however, the managers appreciated the truth despite their hardships.

As a pastor, it is tempting to inflate attendance and giving numbers to fellow pastors. In our current church we are experiencing healthy growth we did not have in my first two years here. It is hard to say that people are leaving, money is down, and the work is hard. A leader's pride can tempt him or her to exaggerate performance and paint a false picture of current conditions. When that happens, leadership integrity is compromised, and the church or organization suffers.

The Devil is the father of lies, which should be enough warning for us to know where lying will lead if we do it. Leaders have to be tactful and confidential but we do not have to lie.

When God gave this Commandment to Moses, it was more specific than a general injunction against lying. We are not to lie against another person. A lie is a lie no matter how it is told but, in particular, God warns Moses that when a person lies about another person, relationships are destroyed and ultimately Israel would be affected.

A leader's core character is honesty and integrity, so lying about anything is uncalled for, especially lying about another person. *Great leaders do not lie; ever.* They tell the truth about their lives, their work, their people, and their experiences. They do not gossip or listen to it because gossip is passive lying (that is reporting or repeating information that you do not know as true).

10. Be Content: "You shall not covet."

Every leader walks a fine line between contentment and a vision to be better. On the one hand, we are commanded to be content and not to envy or covet what anyone else may do, possess, or achieve. It is clear when God calls us to our tasks, He provides us with what we need to accomplish those tasks. We may not have everything we want but we will have what we need. It is sometimes difficult to see another's success when things are going badly in our lives. When you see others who always seem to have more than enough resources, better compensation, easier tasks, and better results, it is hard not to wish for what they have.

Our strength comes from trusting the Lord with what He provides and learning the contentment of trusting Him in all things. Coveting is in the end idolatry because we demand of God what we determine is best for us, thus elevating ourselves above Him.

Being content does not mean that we cannot have visions and dreams for our people, our churches or organizations, however. It is the nature of evangelism and discipleship to see people change and grow. We want our organizations to improve on performance, expand toward the possibilities, and grow in influence. To be ambitious for the things God has given to us is good stewardship and it is the satisfying part of ministry and work.

A leader's responsibility is to make a difference, a positive difference that improves everything under his leadership. Comparisons with others and getting ideas from successful people are fine as long as we apply what we learn to our work without envy and jealousy for what anyone else has.

Envy brings constant discontentment and eventually destroys a leader's focus and joy. It will arrest any creativity, destroy relationships, and undermine a leader's effectiveness. If you envy someone or something they have, you will eventually verbalize it. The words you use, no matter how carefully chosen, will communicate to others your discontentment. People have great difficulty following an unfocused, envious leader because they are unsure of his commitment to them and their enterprise. Also, verbal envy is in reality criticism of those you lead and the things that you have stewardship over; it is very damaging.

Envy is something we can deny ourselves and contentment is something that we have to learn. When the temptation to envy arises, deny the impulse. Then learn the value of practicing contentment by:

- Thanking God for what you have.
- Trusting Him for what you need.

* Asking Him to give you a grateful spirit.
* Asking Him to bless those who seem to have what you want.
* Refusing to verbalize your envious thoughts and feelings.
* Doing your work with confidence in God to provide all you need.

THE TWO BEST CORE LEADERSHIP VIRTUES

I once had the opportunity to visit a military base where officers were trained for potential promotion to their next grade. It was fascinating to meet with men and women who were highly motivated, loyal patriots, and very skilled in leadership. I was fortunate to meet two individuals who had designed the curriculum for those in the program.

We talked about leadership, training people, motivating people, and how difficult it is to predict if a person will be a successful leader. I was intrigued by the various ways the two had designed leadership training, attempting to identify potential leaders and those who might not make the next grade. When I asked them about the characteristics of a great leader, their answer surprised me.

I thought they might give a list of five or ten characteristics of great leaders but they offered only two: *humility and persistence*. One of the men explained that he had spent years researching every general officer in the history of the U.S. Army. He examined (as best he could) their lives and careers, including their assignments during war and times of peace. His conclusion was that the greatest leaders were men of remarkable humility as well as persistence to comply with any order they received.

Humility

I questioned him about the egos of some of the great leaders that I could recall and he admitted that most of them had strong egos but that they also felt and often verbalized a true sense of humility; humility to be privileged to serve their country, to be promoted to leadership above their friends, and to be given strategic opportunities. Many were humbled to have been educated at the U.S. Military Academy and some expressed humility for being cared for by the people of the United States. Their pride did not ruin their true thankfulness and humility for the positions they held.

I think of Moses when I think of humility. His humility is legendary and likely was not surpassed until Christ came to Earth.

"Now Moses was very humble, more than any man who was on the face of the earth." (Numbers 12:3)

What makes Moses' humility so inviting is the strength of his character and the leadership that he displayed. Humility reveals strength in ways that pride, hubris, and selfishness cannot. Humble people are the strong individuals. They have a core strength that will not allow circumstances, criticism, and opposition to defeat them.

True humility is knowing who you are, what your gifts are, and what you can do without pride or condescension. It is being aware of how much grace God has given you in Christ and what He has given you to accomplish. Then you go out and attempt to do it every day.

Humble leaders attract persons to them because they are transparent, trustworthy, and possess a power and authority to do what they say. Great leaders lead without fear; fear of what they are given to accomplish, fear of failure, and fear of people. Their humility is a great strength because they know that it is God who works and has called them to join Him to accomplish His purposes.

It is better to be humble than to act humble and it is better to humble yourself than to be humbled by God. He will not share His glory with another and if we try to claim it for ourselves then He will discipline us and teach us that He is God and we are but His servants. Nearly every leader goes through the experience of being humbled by God. Through failure, rejection, or embarrassment God shows us who He is and who we are in His sight.

Persistence

In the matter of persistence, I was told that the best generals simply would comply with an order no matter their circumstances. He said that these men would not make excuses, they made do with the resources they had on hand, and they would subject themselves to a superior no matter what they thought about an order or command. Their persistence was a characteristic of their entire career from the time they were junior officers until they retired as generals

The persistence of officers who will lead soldiers into battle or who trained soldiers in peacetime meant everything to the success our military has enjoyed. Battles where the odds were against them were won, training when more and better material would have benefited was completed, and in the end everything and everyone improved. These individuals would not quit until the task was done.

I think persistence and its cousin perseverance are two of the greatest and hardest character virtues to develop. Life is hard enough but Kingdom work is at times excruciating. To lead the people of God to fulfill the Great Commission in a world so set against our Lord is nothing short of war. The heart to keep fighting, hoping, believing, and working hard is sometimes our greatest challenge.

I remember hearing Dr. Jerry Falwell say, "For every good day I have as a pastor, I generally have two bad ones." He was not lamenting a hard life but honestly stating how difficult it is to be a Christian leader. There are conflicts, disappointments, seasons of struggle, and heartaches to deal with daily. It seems as if the world is against you (and it is) when you live in righteousness and for righteous things. Often when we preach, no one seems moved; when we communicate, no one seems impressed; when we counsel, people refuse to follow our wisdom; and when we plan great things, no one supports us. And that sometimes feels normal!

I still have difficulties believing I'm having difficulties. But when I think of Moses, I am encouraged. He struggled to lead the Israelites to the Promised Land as they rejected his leadership, they refused to believe God, and they complained about their free food and pure drinking water. They went to the very border of the land God had promised to give them and refused to go in to take possession of it. In fact, they tried to organize themselves and return to Egypt!

Through it all, however, Moses persisted. He lost his temper at times and grew weary with the people but he never stopped leading them. When they refused to enter the Promised Land his leadership did not end. He made adjustments and worked with what he had until the people were prepared to possess their inheritance in Canaan.

Thoughts about quitting what God has given us to complete are not uncommon among leaders. The struggle to implement the Kingdom agenda and achieve Kingdom results is great and takes everything within us. Persistence is what separates true champions from competitors.

Persistence and perseverance are qualities that must be developed through practice in the heat of our battles. We do not need either one until conflicts arise, problems develop, and opposition shows up. We develop endurance in the fires of our testing as leaders by:

* Trusting in God to empower us to stand firm against anything that comes against us or our people.
* Obeying His will no matter the cost or consequences to us personally.
* Remembering what He called us to do, where He sent us to do it, and that it was God Himself who gave us our present task(s).

Fear and discouragement are natural emotions that come to us when we face pressure of conflict, but they are not supernatural gifts. God does not want us to be afraid and He wants us to take courage from Him.

In Moses we see another key leadership principle: *Great leaders are humble and persistent.* I once heard it said that the true measure of a man is whatever it takes to discourage him. How about you? What does it take to discourage you? What do you fear right now? Trust the Lord and exercise the strength He gives you to overcome your doubts and fears.

Chapter Four

—ⲟⲩⲟ—

Communication

I cannot imagine a book on leadership that would not include some reference to communication. As I have already said, leaders talk. They talk constantly because it is a vital part of leadership. Without effective communication the persons we lead do not know what the vision is for their work, what outcomes are anticipated, how the work will get organized and completed, and why they have to do what they do.

Every leader communicates but not every leader communicates well. I think one reason some leaders are poor communicators is that they do not know what to communicate. Ecclesiastes 3:7 reminds us that *"there is a time to be silent and a time to speak."* While I could not agree more, the tough part is knowing what to do when. What needs to be said when is a difficult decision a leader makes constantly.

There are certain communication tasks that you must do, which include:

* A clear understanding of Who you serve—the Lord,
* A clear statement of what He wants done—the vision,
* A clear picture of where you are going—the destination,

* A clear estimation of when you will finish—the time frame,

* A clear outline of how the work will be done—the journey, and

* A clear reason for why you are doing this—the motivation.

Moses communicated each of these to the Israelites and to Pharaoh. God shaped his message and vision. He commanded Moses to demand that Pharaoh release the Hebrews in order for them to go away to Canaan. The time frame was immediate and the motivation was obvious as they left behind their suffering for the land of milk and honey.

A friend of mine put it well when he said to me, "Gene, everyone in every organization needs a compelling image of an achievable future." Without clarity, people become confused and eventually reinterpret the vision itself. Your people will implement either what you have clearly stated or what they have understood through their own interpretation; therefore, effective communication is crucial for successful leadership.

Moses overcame his lack of self-esteem, lack of knowledge, and fear of failure to become a great communicator. He defeated his great fear of stuttering or not speaking well to become the people's voice before Pharaoh and Jehovah.

When God called him to lead the Israelites out from Egypt, Moses had a clear idea of what he was to do. He was to go to Pharaoh with a demand to leave immediately and he was to go to the people to declare to them what God was about to do for them. In the course of time he communicated how they were to prepare, where they were going, why God was doing these things. and where their journey would take them.

There are some things to keep in mind when you communicate with the persons you lead.

* When you communicate you must use clear, concise language. Using too many metaphors, unfamiliar terms, and complicated thoughts and concepts will slow down any process you need

to reach your vision. People cannot do what they do not understand.

* When you have developed your message you must share it over and over again. People do not hear what you say at first. Trust me on this one. It takes multiple times delivering the same message before people begin to comprehend. They always hear but rarely listen at first.

* Adjust your message as you meet milestones on your way to achieving your vision. Once something is done, refer to it but move on to the next stage of the journey.

* Periodically evaluate your church's or organization's progress. It is your job to define reality, which includes your results, good or bad. If current results are poor then you must return to the *who, what, where, when, how,* and *why* of your dreams and goals. These are the foundation stones for your work.

* Communicating a vision is not the same as preaching or instructing. The time you do it may be on a Sunday morning but you are not simply giving facts and motivating people. You are engaging in the process of communication—a process that is not over when the service concludes.

* Communicate in as many arenas as possible. Large gatherings, small groups, lunches, and casual conversation. Fit your message to your audience but communicate it as often as you can.

Do not be surprised if your people do not understand your message the first few times you communicate it. Moses discovered that his delivering God's message to Pharaoh and the Israelites and their receiving that message were two different things. Pharaoh was unimpressed when it was reported to him that the Lord demanded the release of His people.

> *"Who is the Lord that I should obey His voice to let Israel go?
> I do not know the Lord, and besides, I will not let Israel go."*
> (Exodus 5:2)

The reception Moses got from the people was no better.

"May the Lord look upon you and judge you, for you have made us odious in Pharaoh's sight and in the sight of his servants, to put a sword in their hand to kill us." (Exodus 5:21)

Their response was not exactly a victory song anticipating the triumph of the Lord over their enemies! Moses was unsure if God's purposes would ever be successful.

"But Moses spoke to the Lord, saying, 'behold, the sons of Israel have not listened to me; how then will Pharaoh listen to me; for I am unskilled in speech.'" (6:12)

A leader can anticipate predictable stages in communication, each of which will lead to the next if handled properly. They include:

STAGE ONE: INITIAL COMMUNICATION

This is your first attempt at communicating your vision and its tasks. Understand that what you say and what your people hear may be very different. You will likely be excited about a new vision or direction that you see ahead. Your people will likely be anxious about the ways that any coming change might affect them.

I remember an employee meeting I prepared for once where I was about to announce several new initiatives for our division. Included in the initiatives would be some reorganization, new assignments, promotions for some people, closing down some departments, and new measurements to gauge our success.

A consultant was helping me prepare and when we reviewed what I planned to deliver, he cautioned me, saying, "Remember that this meeting will only be the first of many times you will have to deliver your message. Your people won't be listening to much of what you want them to hear." I was stunned and told him so. I had delivered messages to audiences for twenty years as a pastor and was certain that I could deliver what I wanted to say clearly. He said he did not doubt my ability to deliver the message but he did feel certain that my people would not understand it the first time. He went on to say that most of them only wanted to know, one, whether they would have jobs and, two, for whom they would work.

I delivered my speech that day to a rapt audience and we followed it up with focus groups to see what employees heard and understood. There were about ten groups of seven to ten persons in each group who met immediately after the meeting. We carefully constructed questions to see if I had communicated clearly and included in the response sheets places for their questions and concerns. Guess what? Outside of my immediate managers who had been working on the project, hardly anyone understood what we wanted to do or why. And can you imagine what their two chief concerns were? Will I have a job and who will I work for?

It takes hundreds (that's right, hundreds) of hours and opportunities of communicating before people truly understand the vision and purpose of doing what God wants you to lead them to accomplish.

Remember how Moses resisted what God wanted him to do initially? He gave excuses and asked God to get someone else to do it. It took some time and further discussion before he was convinced that he should go to Pharaoh. Do not be surprised if your initial attempts to communicate what God is doing are misunderstood, confuse your folks, and are even rejected by your hearers.

Stage Two: Agreement or Buy-In

It may sound obvious that people will have to agree to do what you ask them to do, but it is not as easy as it sounds. I am a preacher but may I tell you that I struggle with communication? I do not always have the patience to wait for folks to buy in to what I understand to be God's will for us. When I have spent time in prayer, thought, Bible study, and discussions with staff and key laymen in our church, determining a direction I feel the Lord is leading us to follow, I want people to get the message and agree with me so we can get going. If only life were so easy.

Buy-in includes understanding all the elements of what you are going to do, especially the *why* of the endeavor. When your people finally understand the *what* and *why* of something, then they have to make personal commitments of time, money, and hard work. This usually involves accepting some changes that will affect them. Finally, people will accept leadership for what they understand to benefit them, their church, or the organization they serve.

Buy-in is really permission to go forward. Every leader needs it by a majority of those who serve, follow, or work for you. We like to think of ourselves as strong persons who need little or no permission to do God's will but without buy-in from those we lead we will fail.

The key to getting permission is communication. You have to communicate your message hundreds of time (didn't I already say this?) until persons understand, believe, and agree to do what you ask.

In Exodus 24:3 after Moses had given them the initial laws and guidelines from God for their lives, the people answered with one voice, and said, "All the words which the Lord has spoken we will do!" They understood that the God who was speaking to them through Moses and guiding them had a purpose for them and could be trusted. They bought into who He was, what He wanted, and how He would lead them. They did not keep their commitment perfectly but it was the beginning of their buy-in to their destiny.

Your people's initial buy-in to the vision God has for you will come sooner or later. When it does it is a great step forward for your leadership. Your communication does not end at this point, however. Like Moses, you will discover that God's people are not always as faithful and true to their commitments to Him and to their leaders as they intend to be. So keep communicating and keep bringing the folks along.

STAGE THREE: OWNERSHIP

Ownership begins when your people can articulate the *who, what, where, when, how,* and *why* clearly, with passion and excitement. It is in full force when they join with you to do the work necessary to complete the task. It reaches its most powerful dynamic when your folks come to you with ideas of their own to make things better.

When you lead people well, they will work long hours, make tremendous sacrifices, and persist until the job gets done. Ownership of a project or movement is one of the greatest rewards a leader enjoys. The burden of the work is shared and the joys of the vision are multiplied. God is honored through your leadership and through the people's labor.

During this stage in the process, communication changes from convincing folks to join you to encouraging and thanking them for what they are accomplishing.

Exodus and the books that follow reveal how the Israelites gradually understood more and more of who they were and what God wanted. Eventually priests and judges were appointed to serve in their roles. Moses appointed seventy leaders to assist him in the daily administration of the people's needs. Despite the many times the people failed to understand or obey God, over time they became a nation ready to move into the land God had promised to Abraham.

Be sure to lead your people in such a way that they eventually own God's vision for them and live in that vision—to see it accomplished.

GETTING IT RIGHT

Right now you may be thinking that you serve a small church or lead a small organization that will not require all these things. I know how you feel and I know how unproductive those feelings are. In fact, it really doesn't matter how large or small your congregation or entity is—you still have to communicate with your people. It is one of your most important tasks, so why not do it well? I imagine you have people in your church who have heard sermons all their lives on how God wants them to live but you keep preaching and teaching biblical truths to them weekly. You have preached sermons on evangelism or church growth many times but you still have folks who won't witness or read their Bibles. So you keep preaching and teaching them.

Some things that might help you to become a great communicator are:

* Write down what you want to communicate. Then rewrite it until it is simple and clear. Think about how your message will be understood by the youngest, newest, and most inexperienced listener.

* Speak to as many people in as many groups as possible. Vary the venues by size and age as much as possible. Do not be afraid to mix younger persons with older ones.

* Get feedback from every group. Select persons who will give you honest evaluations of what you communicate. Never try to force their opinions or answers and don't be disappointed with what they say. Remember, the bad news is the good news because you can fix it.

* If possible, record your presentations. It may be painful at first but this will help you evaluate your message, tone, pace of speaking, and voice inflections. Listen to yourself and determine to get better the next time you speak.

God has called you to lead your people and He called you by communicating to you. You have prayed, read Scripture, and consulted with your leaders about this vision He has given you for your people. Why not commit to clearly communicate to them the details of what God wants done? Be patient with them until they understand. Spend time listening to their concerns and try to answer their questions honestly. Do not be afraid to define reality for them and encourage them to change their minds. If you believe God has set you up and given you a task, then commit to get it done no matter how long it takes or how hard it is.

Moses' experience teaches us that *great leaders communicate clear messages over and over and over...*

Chapter Five

—◦◦◦—

The Leader and His People

If I had to name only one issue that can potentially destroy a leader it would be the issue of relationships. Many years ago I read the results of an extensive study of pastors, staff members, missionaries, and leaders of Christian organizations. The study focused on what it takes to successfully start a ministry and bring it to maturity. I found the findings interesting and not too surprising, but one thing got my attention and it has made an indelible impression on me and my ministry.

The study found that most persons in ministry had a clear calling from God which they gladly fulfilled even if it called for great sacrifices. The study results also noted that most persons in ministry received great satisfaction from doing what God called them to do. They willingly put in great amounts of effort and time to do their work; and they generally enjoyed it. But the last finding really got my attention. The study found that while most ministers felt a keen sense of calling and enjoyed doing what they did *they did not like the people they worked with daily*!

Can you believe it? Leaders don't enjoy the people they are called to serve and serve with! Not only can we believe it, we know it's often true. One of the reasons this has made such an impression on my life is because, at the time I read the study, I was totally exasperated with some of my church leaders and the staff I was currently serving with. I am called to preach and pastor. I am never more me than when I am preaching, teaching, witnessing, praying, and developing a God-given vision for our church. But sometimes those people...

RELATIONSHIPS

Your spiritual core describes you and helps you function as a leader. Your character guides your thinking, decision-making, and focus. It keeps you from wrong and leads you to the right. Your relationships are the places where you come to life and function.

I believe that relationships are the key to life. Your relationships with God, your spouse, your children and grandchildren, your friends, and your people are the reasons for your life. We were created to know God and to be with others. Why are relationships so often difficult and unpleasant? I do not know how you might answer that question but I have a few answers I'll offer.

* Some people are unkind, untrustworthy, and mean. If you have been hurt, thrown under the bus or run over lately, you know what I am saying.

* It's hard to get to know people because everyone is busy. This is true and with today's communication gadgets it makes serious conversation harder and time a premium.

* I have so many people I deal with I don't know where to start. "Amen!" you say. I sometimes think that if I have to deal with another question, listen to another "let-me-help-you" conversation, look at another grandchild's picture, or deal with another problem I might lose it. Okay, it's my job and I enjoy it most times, but sometimes I'd like to check out for a while.

Relationships are also difficult because I am not perfect and I do not always behave in ways that make it easy for others to like me or to understand what I am trying to say and do. But no matter how challenging or frustrating they may be, relationships are crucial.

Your Relationship with God

The key to how you relate to others is how you relate to your Heavenly Father through Jesus Christ. It is in Christ that we learn who we really are and what our purpose in this life is. Time with the Lord renders wisdom, discernment, assurance, and faith to minister. The closer I am to the Father the more courage, strength, vision, and power I have. On my own I am nothing, possess nothing, and can do nothing. But in Christ the Father can use me in great ways to fulfill His purposes in this world.

I have found over the years that spending time with the Father:

* gives me more time for a balanced life with family, work, friends, and personal time.
* gives me more patience and understanding in dealing with difficult persons.
* gives me more power and authority to fulfill my Kingdom obligations.
* opens up more opportunities to share Christ, encourage hurting persons, and give help to people in need.
* makes it unnecessary to worry about church giving, attendance, or whether our church sign is working. Plus I sleep better.

In other words, spending time with the Lord is to be enabled to meet the demands of every day and the days to come. I am certain that my capacity for good relationships is a direct result of being with Him.

I think Moses experienced the same thing. When he left the Lord's presence His glory shone on his face and he had power and authority to lead the Israelites through the next crisis or to their next location. *Time alone with the Lord is the key to good relationships.*

Time with the Lord is the foundation for good relationships but
our relationships with people have many dimensions. From Moses'
experience alone I can think of a large number of roles he had in
relating to the Israelites. They included:

* leader,
* historian/writer,
* law-giver,
* spokesman/communicator,
* commander-in-chief of the Israelite army,
* judge,
* theologian/spiritual leader,
* fundraiser,
* construction manager,
* intercessor, and
* disciplinarian.

These are the ones that come immediately to mind. In his various
roles, Moses related to various individuals and groups and each group
required a different type of leadership.

OPPOSITION, OBSTACLES, AND ENEMIES

Pharaoh is a classic example of how a leader must relate to and deal
with an enemy or obstacle. Every leader faces opposition in the form
of persons, groups, forces, laws, movements, etc. It is a part of leadership to lead people through opposition, obstructions, and obstacles.
Moses faced Pharaoh with many obstacles but Moses had to face
Pharaoh in order to lead the Israelites out of Egypt.

It is important to know what persons or forces are against you, to
take them seriously, and to meet them as soon as you can with all the
strength you have. Nothing gets done until the enemies, opposition,

and obstacles are conquered. It may take little time or a long time but we learn from Moses that obstructions to God's will and His plans must be overcome.

Do not be discouraged when you face opposition. It is to be expected from within and without. Moses had to quell rebellions (Numbers 14:1–35), quiet attempts to undermine his leadership (Numbers 12:1–15), resist Pharaoh and his army, and respond to nations like the Amalekites (Exodus 17:8–16) and the Amorites (Numbers 21:21–32).

As a leader, you must not be surprised or discouraged when you face opposition. It comes with change or when you challenge the status quo. Expecting opposition, however, is not the same thing as enjoying it. No leader enjoys opposition or obstructions that threaten the vision that God has given him. Many times we lead our people in the face of stubborn, powerful, and formidable resistance. If God is guiding you as a leader to accomplish His will, you are assured of victory over any resistance. You are not excused from the struggle nor from expending all your spiritual, mental, and physical energy. Courage is faith put to the test under fire, when we determine to face our fears and do what God wants.

When Moses doubted his success God said to him,

> *"Now you shall see what I will do to Pharaoh; for under compulsion he shall let them go, and under compulsion he shall drive them out of his land."* (Exodus 6:1)

By the time God was about to send the tenth plague, Scripture notes,

> *"Furthermore, the man Moses himself was greatly esteemed in the land of Egypt, both in the sight of Pharaoh's servants and in the sight of the people."* (11:3)

You must remember that it is the Lord who is working through you to accomplish His purposes. There is no reason to believe that you will not overcome your opposition as long as you are fulfilling His will.

Great leaders meet opposition with strength of character and the power of their calling and vision. Not everyone we lead or meet or confront is a friend and ally. There are mean people everywhere who must be dealt with. Trust God to give you wisdom and courage to meet them with His strength and power. He will provide what you need in these situations but you must use what He gives you to confront your opposition.

FAMILY

We know little of Moses' family. His wife was Zipporah, one of Jethro's seven daughters, and his two sons were Gershom and Eliezer. We know more about his father-in-law, Jethro, who gave him a job tending his flocks when Moses fled Egypt. Jethro kept Moses' family safe for him while he was in Egypt confronting Pharaoh and returned them to him when Israel went into the wilderness. We cannot project into Moses' time and life some of the principles of marriage and family that we enjoy today. But we can see that, in his life, family was important to him in a remarkable way. He protected Zipporah and the children when he returned to Egypt. Although they returned with him initially, in time they returned to Jethro's protection. Moses wanted to insure their safety.

He respected his wife's father and family. He met Zipporah and her sisters at a well when he stood up to some shepherds who were intimidating them as they watered their father's flock (Exodus 2:16–17). Moses did what he should have done as a man by protecting the women from harm and from unfair treatment. Years later, Moses asked Jethro if he could return to Egypt to see about his family, showing deep respect for Jethro and for his wife (Exodus 4:18).

We know that Moses and Jethro had tremendous respect for each other. Moses recognized Jethro's wisdom when he told him how to organize judges to help him resolve the Israelites' disputes. Moses invited Hobab his brother-in-law to go with them on their journey and offered Hobab the same blessings that the Israelites would receive from the Lord.

Moses did what a husband, father, and family member should do, that is, he did the right thing. He provided for his family through hard work, he protected his family from real and potential danger, he respected his family by taking the advice of Jethro, and he was generous to his family by offering to take Hobab and his family to the Promised Land.

A leader must have a core foundation to build his relationships with his family successfully. You are unique as a person and you have a unique assignment from God. That means that your relationship with your family is unique to you and to them. But you must realize that when God calls you to an assignment, He calls your family, your spouse, and your children. He does not call you to break your family apart in order to serve Him.

A man provides for and protects his wife and children under God's authority. He serves them not as an organizational leader but as a loving, caring husband and father. A woman respects her husband and encourages him. She loves and nurtures her children so they can grow up in an environment that is loving and secure. A leader's strong marriage is the fundamental influence upon the children. Putting their interests before his own allows him to do what is best for them. There are always obligations upon a leader that put pressure on his life as he serves the Lord. But those obligations are never reasons or excuses for neglecting our families.

We see that Moses took care of his family.

ASSOCIATES AND HELPERS

As we have noted, Moses benefited from many persons who helped him lead Israel successfully. Aaron was his spokesman and the first priest appointed to lead Israel in worship. Jethro was his counselor and supporter when he initially led Israel from Egypt. Joshua was his trusted servant who led the Israelites in battle, was one of the spies, and one who always stayed close by Moses' side.

Moses appointed judges to help him settle disputes and he appointed seventy choice elders who helped him lead the people. These administrators were indispensable to him because they would help Moses *"bear the burdens of the people with you"* (Numbers 11:16–17). The responsibility for the people of God was Moses' responsibility but the burdens and duties of seeing their needs met was shared with these seventy men. What we see in Moses' leadership is that he selected the men for leadership, he instructed (trained and mentored) them, clarified their work, let them do their jobs, and he held them accountable for what he expected. There were also various other helpers he depended on to organize the twelve tribes in marching order, craftsmen to construct the tabernacle, and various other leaders like the *"two hundred fifty leaders of the congregation, chosen in the assembly, men of renown"* (Numbers 16:2).

In addition to leading these leaders, Moses had to confront them when they rebelled against his leadership. No leader likes to imagine a situation when his staff or management team stages an open and active rebellion against him—but it happens. We learn from Moses that not only does a leader develop a leadership team to help him but he also disciplines anyone who rebels against his authority or undermines the work that must be done to accomplish the vision God has given him.

We read in Numbers 16 of a rebellion led by three men, Korah, Dathon, and Abiram who in turn enlisted the above mentioned two hundred fifty men of renown to overthrow Moses. They accused him before the people of exalting himself above the people. Moses was quick to respond and told them what they must do to see if God would support their claims. Of course, the Lord did not support them and they all died for their rebellion when the Lord consumed them.

It is important to note that Moses did not take this personally in the sense that he wanted revenge for what they tried to do to him. He wanted God to deal with the three men who had falsely accused him. But Moses immediately confronted them and settled the issue fast. There is never a reason to wait to deal with problems. We cannot make them go away by ignoring them or letting fear immobilize us.

My father taught me a valuable leadership lesson when I was young. A man worked for him who would not follow safety instructions while operating a machine. I worked as a summer employee at the same company but not in the same division as my father. I overheard the man telling another employee that my dad had told him to stop operating the machine unsafely but he was going to do it anyway. Someone (not me) told my dad what the employee had said. That afternoon I saw Daddy walking from his office to where the man was working. I could not hear what was said but the conversation was short. When my father finished, he walked away and the man left the machine, got into his truck, and drove away.

At dinner that evening I asked my dad about what had happened. He responded without much emotion and said, "When you have a problem with a person, it's best to take care of it immediately. I told him what I wanted; he refused, which created a problem that I took care of right away."

A leader soon realizes that people problems do not get better. Do not take the issue personally. Remember that God has called you to accomplish something for Him. If there are those on your staff or team who do not agree, who refuse to help you, or rebel against your leadership, then you must act quickly to settle the issue. Sometimes people repent or change their minds about who you are and what you want. There are other times when they refuse and have no place to serve with you. The sooner you take care of such issues, the better off you will be.

THE PEOPLE YOU LEAD

One of the most difficult decisions a leader makes is how to relate to the people he or she leads. Is it possible to be friends with your staff or team and the persons in your church or organization? Is it wise to

be friendly with some of the people you like and not with others you
do not like?

Leadership requires that you be able to lead people by making
important decisions, assessing your current environment, defining
reality for your people, and implementing tough choices when necessary. These are a few things leaders must do in order to accomplish
the tasks and assignments God gives them.

Great leaders are accessible, honest, easy to talk to, open to ideas,
and eager to help their people accomplish their tasks. But there is a
line between a leader and his people that cannot be crossed without
risking failure. That line may not be easy to define but it is there and
must be recognized. It keeps a leader in leadership, which means that
he or she can do what leaders do without being compromised.

I have heard some say that leaders should not be close to their
people and others say just the opposite. Who is right? I do not think
it is reasonable for a leader not to interact with his people but nor is
it helpful to become so engaged with them that he cannot lead. God's
call establishes your priorities and your assignment includes relating
to your people. But your leadership cannot be a servant to your relationships or it will not be effective.

That is the point; if your relationships with your people com-
promise or negatively affect your leadership then you must change
something. We have already established that there will be opposition
(sometimes from your own people), conflicts, and issues that must
be resolved. There will be times when you have to tell your favorite
person or most productive associate something they will not like. You
will have times when you have to correct or discipline a staff member
or a person in your congregation. There will be seasons when you will
have to deliver some bad or unwelcome news to your people—news
that will make them angry or sad. It happens and if your relationship
with them prevents your doing it then you have lost your ability to
lead.

Moses is a good model to follow because he was always focused
on the task God had given him and the people he led. He interceded

with God for the people and he represented the Lord to the people. He never let anything prevent him from hearing from God or leading God's people. For Moses it was all about the Lord and all about the people. He communicated truthfully to the people no matter the subject or news. He walked with integrity and did not let any relationship destroy his leadership. He could be harsh when necessary as with Aaron in the incident with the golden calf or he could be gentle and heartbroken as when he pleaded with God to spare the people.

Moses never stopped leading the people no matter how little they understood or cared for what he was doing. He had a mission and he was going to complete it. He knew what God wanted and what it took to do it—so he did it. Nothing distracted Moses from fulfilling his task.

If you remember that you work for God and serve His people, then your life will stay in clear focus. A good leader is friendly, transparent, open, consistent, and loves his people. That is not the same as saying that you are just like them because you are not. God called you to serve His purposes by serving others but that makes you different from those you lead. You are not smarter, better, or more spiritual—but you are different. That difference makes you a leader.

GETTING A GRIP ON LEADERSHIP

It is likely that if you have read this far you are in a situation where you are trying to determine how to lead your people to accomplish something. It may be that they either do not understand what you want to do or even that they do not want to do it. Change for people is hard even for people who are struggling and failing. Your call to lead your people will require the best of what you can be, combined with all of what God can give you.

We must remind ourselves constantly what God has called us to fulfill for His purposes. We must not lose focus and we must not let anything or anyone pull us away from those purposes. Great leaders have a keen sense of purpose, build great relationships that move people toward God's purposes, and keep a perspective on what it takes to be successful.

I am fortunate to have made great friendships through the years in places I have served the Lord. In churches, organizations, corporations, small ministries, boards I served on, and in communities where I have lived. The friends I have made across the years are the real story of my life. I have loved them, served them, and led them as best I could while I was their leader. I have opened my heart to them and shared burdens, dreams, failures, and things that excited me. But never was I excused from leading them.

Great leaders have the privilege of building great friendships over the years without compromising their role of working for God to build His Kingdom.

Chapter Six

—◦◦◦—

Putting the Principles to Work

The principles we have discovered from Moses' life are solid and inspirational. But the time comes when we have to leave the solitude of our thoughts and get to work. How do you take the things we have learned from Moses and put them into practice where you currently serve?

I have outlined some steps that have served me well for the years I have been a servant of the Lord. They are *principles*, so your application of them may differ from mine but they will help you bring God's vision into your life and into the lives of your people. I hope they serve you as well as they serve me.

VISION

Leaders do two primary things that seem to be in opposition but in fact are in concert. Leaders define current reality for their people then they bring changes to that reality, which creates new realities. If a church is in trouble, people may see the need for change or they may resist it. If people in a church or organization do not see the need for change, then conflict usually accompanies a leader's efforts to bring change.

It is important to have a God-given vision. Vision identifies current reality, reveals the need for change, shows the dangers of not changing, and reveals the benefits of changing. In addition, a vision brings a picture of the future that has a compelling power to bring people to it. When people understand the hope and future of change they come to it with a commitment they will meet with sacrifice, devotion, and perseverance.

Moses' experience bears this out. He had a vision from God. The vision was a reality that God Himself gave him but it was also a reality that God was going to accomplish. A God-given vision is very different from a vision a person can develop. Most visions we see from churches to corporations to nonprofit organizations are in fact dreams. They are what we hope happens if things go well. Everyone has dreams but few leaders have visions. When God gives you a vision you can write it down and give your life to it. It may take time, great effort, and enormous patience, but it will happen. When God brings change, conflict is never far behind and spiritual warfare is predictable and it will happen.

Moses reported to the Israelites what God had told him. The elders heard with interest but could not get their minds around it or their hearts in it. Pharaoh simply rejected it and attempted to dismiss it outright. The vision did not change so Moses kept going back, refining his message, and communicating it to Israel and to Pharaoh.

If you are committed to leading your church or organization to a better future, then get your vision from God, trust Him, communicate it to your people, and keep at it. The way to change your church is to clearly know the issues that keep you from being (or from becoming) what God wants you to be. You must be certain of what God wants you to be or become. You must know your church's strengths, weaknesses, opportunities, and what the threats are, and your people must agree with you. You cannot change what you don't know and you should not change anything until you know why.

Moses knew the situation of oppression of the Israelites but God gave him background as to why their current situation would change.

He told Moses that the covenant He had made with Abraham, Isaac, and Jacob could not be broken and God meant to make it good. The people did not understand it initially and Pharaoh had no idea of it, but it was there and it was the basis of God's redemption.

We have no less responsibility than Moses to hear from God about what He is doing and what He wants to do through us. Biblically, a basic framework centers in the Kingdom of God. The Kingdom of God is the fundamental reality in the Universe. The prophets predicted it, John the Baptist announced it, and Jesus inaugurated it and He is fulfilling it right now. This is God's work through Christ who destroyed the work of the devil, defeated death, and is taking back the territory Adam and Eve relinquished to Satan in the Garden of Eden.

KINGDOM

The advance of the Kingdom of God got momentum with God's promise to Abraham and accelerated when Jesus came to Earth, died on the cross, and rose from death. His victory means salvation for God's people and judgment for the world. The birth of the Church as God's Kingdom agent gives a prominence to it that we sometimes miss.

The Kingdom promise was given to Moses in Exodus 19 when God spoke to Him.

"Now then, if you will indeed obey My voice and keep My covenant, then you shall be My own possession among all the peoples, for all the earth is Mine; and you shall be to Me a kingdom of priests and a holy nation." (Exodus 19:5–6)

At the heart of all He is doing, God is establishing the Kingdom and His reign in the lives of His people not only to save them but to use them to accomplish His purposes. The vision you have for your church (or organization) must focus on the Kingdom of God or it is not from the Lord. Christ is building His church in order to build or extend the Father's rule among the nations. Is that your dream?

Do you embrace this vision? Until you do, the rest of your applied leadership may be wasting away. Your energy is good, your intentions are pure, but you are not aligned with what God wants or is doing.

God told Moses plainly that if the people would obey Him and keep His covenant, then the Israelites would be a kingdom of priests and a holy nation. It is God's intention to redeem a people for Himself to represent Him among the nations and to use them for His purposes. This means that He raises up leaders to accomplish those purposes. His will for this world then becomes our visions, our strategies, and our plans. We must hear from the Lord and then respond to Him accordingly. It is God who imagines, purposes, leads, and supplies His people to fulfill His will in this world.

BAD NEWS, GOOD NEWS

You can determine what God's Kingdom demands are by praying, studying Scripture, and having serious discussions with your people. You must then determine what issues you face that either help or hurt meeting those demands. These also must be determined with the help of those in your ministry or the organization. This can be a formidable challenge, especially if you have never done it. But remember that *the bad news is the good news!* That's right, whatever you discover that are weaknesses or threats to your ministry are things that you can begin to address immediately. Furthermore, you will discover that your church's strengths and potential will help you overcome the things that threaten you.

Most leaders do not like to hear bad news. With all that we face every day, more problems can seem overwhelming, but problems are part of the task we've been given. Leaders solve problems and make things better in order to accomplish their missions. It takes courage and faith to face the issues that threaten us, but with courage and faith problems turn into the opportunities we need to be successful.

In one sense, Moses' life experience was a series of problems that he faced as the leader of Israel. He had trouble convincing the people that God would deliver them. He had to keep focused when Pharaoh made their work harder and they grew angry with him. He had a mega-struggle with Pharaoh, constantly demanding that Egypt release the Hebrew people from slavery. Moses had to manage food and water for them as they traveled. He had to deal with idolatry, rebellion, their stubbornness, and constant fear. He faced nations in war and he watched as the Israelites rejected the laws they promised to obey. He lived in constant tension, mediating between Jehovah and His people. Whew!

Kingdom leadership is not for the weak and faint of heart, is it? We need to view Moses' life as a template for our own work. It is a long journey in an ordained direction and in our daily struggle we must not lose sight of the vision or goals. Moses endured his issues every day in order that Israel might eventually arrive in the Land of Promise.

The issues you face and overcome today bring you and your people closer to the destination God has ordained for you. Leadership is as much struggle as it is imagining, communicating, and celebrating. The brief celebrations we enjoy are often won through desperate struggle.

I see another leadership principle here. *You cannot reach the delights of your vision until you meet the demands of your problems.* If you are like me, you do not enjoy problems but I have come to understand that (1) they do not go away on their own and (2) if left alone they get worse. In addition, I know that I cannot give away my problems to anyone else. They are mine and I must deal with them. I can always find people to help me and advise me, but in the end as a leader I must deal with my problems.

Because our problems will not go away until we deal with them, we might as well face them with courage and faith. God has called you to be His leader. The church or organization you serve is His and you are on a Kingdom assignment. He sent you and He will sustain you with whatever you need to meet the demands you face. Trust Him and take courage to do what is necessary and right, with the wisdom and discernment He affords. If you do, things will eventually get better.

Let's be real for a moment. Some of us have been called and sent to some very difficult places. The challenges you may face today may be difficult, threatening, and disheartening. Some churches barely resemble what God has in mind for them. Some organizations struggle constantly with lack of funding, poor employee performance, legal issues, and many such problems. Despite the problems, however, we press on because the ultimate issues are God's to resolve and we are His servants, joining Him in His work. He works victories for His people, through His people. He works through His people by giving them leaders who stand for the Lord and for His people as they face problems, hardships, enemies, and battles.

Take all the time you need to sit with your folks to identify and communicate your vision. Then carefully identify the issues you face that prevent you from reaching it. List the opportunities and strengths you have but be sure to be determined to meet your problems with God's help—and you will.

STRATEGY

There are numerous definitions of strategy, but I suggest a helpful way to look at strategy is to think about what you intend to do to make your dream or vision a reality. These are often called "strategic intents" and they help to frame what needs to be done to get our folks where they need to be in a prescribed amount of time.

God helped Moses set his strategy by giving him the end of the journey first. He outlined His promise to Abraham, Isaac, and Jacob and then acknowledged the suffering of the Israelites in Egypt. But that was not the vision. God's will for His people was more concrete than a long-ago promise or a sympathetic recognition of their slavery. He had an end in mind that required a leader, a journey, and a land. God wanted His people to live in a land that He would provide them. To reach that land, the people would experience a long journey in an ordained direction. Jehovah was their God, Moses their leader, the law their guide, and the wilderness their school to build their faith and obedience.

You are a leader, you have a vision, and now you need a strategy that reveals your intentions—how you will reach your dream. God has called you to Himself, given you His will (your vision) for your people, and assigned you a Kingdom task. When you make God's will your passion, then you come to have ideas about how to accomplish what He wants. Your time with the Lord and with your people will help you clarify what your intentions are, to accomplish the things that need to be done.

Moses spent time with the Lord receiving instructions about what to say and do for the Israelites and from those times came strong leadership. No leader has all the information he wants all the time but decisions still have to be made and implemented. Clearly stated intentions keep you focused when things may not be as you would like. Your vision and your strategy or strategic intentions are the *what* and *where* of what God is calling you and your people to do.

THE MINISTRY PLAN

Ultimately you must determine *how* you are going to reach your vision. These are the steps that must be taken to get things going in the right direction. Reading Exodus reveals a number of important things that Moses had to do in order to get the Israelites moving. He instructed them on how to prepare the Passover, how to prepare to leave Egypt quickly, and how to gather resources from the Egyptians when they left (Exodus 12). Once *en route* he had to organize the people in marching order. He had to give instructions on what to eat, what to do to obey the Lord's commands, and how to prepare themselves to enter their new homeland. These things are the *how* of what must be done to get from Egypt to Canaan.

You must do the same. A leader's task is not only defining what, why, and where, but also how. I personally think that articulating the vision from God is the most difficult task. But I think outlining how the vision is going to be completed is the most tedious. Visions are big pictures with compelling images of a better future everyone desires. Plans to reach that vision are the details we often get lost in when we lead. Not paying attention to details is a sure formula to fail.

Moses communicated a variety of things to the Israelites. He gave them grandiose pictures of a land filled with milk and honey, vineyards, and fields ripe for harvest, clear water, and houses. He also commanded them in detail about how to worship, how to build the tabernacle, and what to eat. Some say that leadership is about vision and management is about the details of work to achieve the vision. In reality leadership is both and you need to do both well. Just like the problems we would rather avoid, most of us would rather leave the details to others. It is necessary to delegate details to others but you cannot release your responsibility for those details to be done well.

WORK, PEOPLE, ALIGNMENT, AND OBSTACLES

Work

A part of the task of how to get things done will revolve around what work has to be done, who will do the work, how will the people be aligned (organized) to do the work, and what obstacles must be overcome to be successful.

Have you determined the work your people must do this week in order to move to the place the Lord wants them? Can you tell weekly or daily if they are doing what needs to be done to fulfill the Great Commission? Are you working on the things that count for the Kingdom? Have you put your people in the right alignment for them to be successful? If you haven't, then how will you know if they are doing well? How will they know?

If you determine to move your folks to a God-given vision (or place), then what will they have to do to get there today, this week, this year? These are important considerations that will keep you and your people working on essential things and avoiding trivial ones.

The goal of our leadership is to make it as easy and simple as possible for your people to live for Christ and serve His purposes. If your vision is to fulfill the Great Commission, are you and your people working to that end? Identify the details of the work that must be done, the details of what work is being done, and then make adjustments to stop what doesn't help and start what does.

People

Another task is to determine the gifts and readiness of your people for what must be done. You might remember in a previous chapter that we talked about the number of times you must communicate the vision to people. Until people understand what God is leading them to accomplish, they will not work to accomplish it.

One of my traits that has not always served me well is an optimism that people I lead are willing to do what I want done in the ways I want it done. I believe it is a chronic condition many leaders face, called "leader's optimism." We are called by God to accomplish a Kingdom task and we are energized about what might be accomplished. We see clearly the wisdom of what God wants and the path to take to reach that vision. We spend time in prayer and Bible study, searching the mind of God for His will. Like Moses, we go to the mountain of God frequently and we hear from Him. We come away from those times assured of His presence and His will for our churches and organizations. We brood over what we see as issues both positive and negative and how we are going to lead our people to the success the vision promises. We even talk about it with some folks and they seem interested and perhaps even excited.

The moment comes when all of our reservations about what God wants have melted away. Our personal fears and doubts have been resolved and we are ready to move. We stand before our people with the exciting news that God has spoken, changes are coming, and a new journey is beginning, and we deliver this news expecting a joyous commitment from those people. But so often their response ranges from confusion to outright rebellion. We are stunned that they are so sinfully unexcited. We feel rejected, frustrated, taken back, and perhaps angry.

What just happened? A clear case of "leader's optimism," assuming that everything we were thinking our folks were thinking. Unless you are in a remarkable situation or have been with your people a long, long time, it rarely happens like that.

Moses experienced this nearly every time he met with the Lord and received instructions from Him. The people rarely understood it the first time or bought into what he said. One of the best gifts you can give yourself is a realistic view of the people you lead. You may not like what you see but they are who they are right now. You can lead them to change but you have to start where they are right now. Their first steps to the work required to reach the vision may be small and you may even be disappointed that things are not going faster, but your persistence will eventually pay off. If you understand the details of their work then you can help them do it. Remember how Jethro advised Moses to tell the people what they were to do and then show them how to do it? People can and will learn almost anything when they understand what you want them to do and why you want them to do it. Kingdom work is not difficult, just important.

I think a good leadership principle to remember is: *Kingdom leaders assess their people objectively, to determine their strengths and weaknesses for doing the work required to reach their vision.*

Alignment

We have to get people aligned in their work or chaos will be our master. Organization includes more than lines and boxes on paper or a media presentation. It includes the following:

* people in relation to other people to do the work,
* time that people have to do the work,
* space to do the work,
* money to fund the work,

* training to do the work, and
* resources or all the "stuff" it takes to do the work.

People have to be in the right relationships, doing the right things, with the right stuff in order to be effective. Organization alone will not bring success (only people can do that), but the wrong alignment can cause failure, create inefficiency, or unduly prolong your processes.

If you do not have a clear vision and clear intentions about what you are going to do to realize your vision, then you cannot organize your work correctly. You will have people in the wrong places, spending time working on things that ultimately don't matter, spending money you cannot afford to waste, trained in the wrong things, and using the wrong "stuff" to little or no avail. Other than that, you don't have any concerns!

It is difficult keeping your people focused on the big picture while taking care of the necessary details to do the right work. But it is a leader's responsibility to ensure that everything is done according to the plans and intentions everyone knows will help you be, do, and accomplish what God desires.

You may not have your vision clearly articulated or perhaps your folks are not completely behind what God wants done, so what should you do? Keep working on developing and articulating the vision and your intentions (the *what* and *why*). Don't stop even though things are not where you want them right now. And work on the work. That is, give attention to knowing your people; where they are, what they think, and what they can do. Analyze your space and your finances. Are you utilizing your space well? Are you spending your money wisely? What about training that your folks need? Do they need new skill sets or more knowledge? Do you need to begin to adjust how you spend your time with them? What about how they are spending their time? Do you need any more or different equipment, tables, computers, or other "stuff"?

You can work on the work right now, so get to work.

Obstacles

We have addressed the reality of the problems that leaders face. Obstacles are in the category of problems experienced and requiring answers. But I want to use obstacles in a different sense than ordinary, troublesome issues that leaders face.

You need to determine what true obstacles may prevent you from realizing your vision. If you are going to grow in attendance in your church, then space is an immediate issue. What will you do to overcome a space shortage? If you don't overcome it, then growth is impossible. If you need more money, how will you raise it? Will you build Kingdom stewards or just raise money?

Will you be able to convince your folks to spend more time on your vision or will they return to their own concerns? Do you have the kind of people who can do (or will be willing to do) the work it will take to accomplish what God is leading you to do?

Overcoming obstacles is a part of leadership. Your creativity will be tested as you face the threats to your vision. When you meet an obstacle, you have to go around, over, under, or through it, especially if you cannot eliminate it completely. Leaders have many things to do simultaneously but dealing with real barriers is one of the important tasks.

Do you remember Moses' most famous obstacle? Right: the Red Sea loomed before the Israelites and Pharaoh's army was in hot pursuit behind them. Moses was not able to relinquish his other duties but he had to deal with the Sea. As an obstacle, I rate it nearly at the top of what any other leader has ever faced.

The scene in Exodus is classic. Moses and the Israelites have left Egypt in a hurry, carrying Joseph's bones, "in martial array," under a pillar of cloud by day and a pillar of fire at night (13:16–22). They marched out to the wilderness and camped there until the Lord told Moses to take the throng to the Red Sea. Things were fine until someone noticed that Pharaoh had changed his mind and sent his army to bring them back.

The people's words were classic. *"Is it because there were no graves in Egypt that you have taken us away to die in the wilderness?"*

(14:11). Giving strength to their fears and criticism of Moses, they asked if he had forgotten when they had said, *"Leave us alone that we may serve the Egyptians"* (14:12).

So much for the optimism a vision creates, huh? An approaching army hems the nation in before the Red Sea, which is an obstacle they cannot walk over, go under, or around. It was an obstacle that seemed impossible to overcome. Moses does what many leaders do when they don't have the answers—he tells the people to stand still and watch for what the Lord will do. As he speaks, the Lord interrupts him and tells him to get the people moving *through the Sea!* That's an option I'm sure no one discussed. But God divides the water, the people walk through the Sea on dry land, and eventually Pharaoh and his army is destroyed.

We can learn a lot about overcoming obstacles here. Yours are yours and mine are mine, but each one we face is keeping us from moving forward. What comes out of this for leaders includes:

* God is working and our enemies and obstacles are no match for what He is doing.
* He will give us wisdom, discernment, power, and authority to overcome our obstacles.
* No matter what God does, we have to join Him in faith to see our obstacles removed.
* The things that threaten us today might be the very thing God will use to destroy your enemies tomorrow.
* God has the power which He gives to His leaders to assist His people to overcome their obstacles.
* God always delivers us on time and never too soon or too late.

Obstacles are real threats to us but they can and will be removed as God works through us to accomplish His will. However, do not try to remove them in your own wisdom and strength. God will give you the wisdom, timing, and resources to overcome them. As you face your obstacles keep moving until God says, "Stop" and start moving when He says, "Go."

Get Going

Learning leadership from Moses is exciting and motivating. You are where you are right now until God leads you away—so get going. Spend time with Him and your confidence in what He is doing and wants done will grow. Spending time with God always helps me to clarify what I am doing. In addition, I find that, as I pray and read Scripture, my fears recede and my faith grows. I find strength to meet my trials.

When God speaks to you, it has a great effect on your people. They will pick up on your vision, your excitement, and your confidence in what God is doing. The changes they see in you will be a catalyst for their own change.

If you are unsure about your present situation and what God wants you to do as a leader, spend some time with Him. In spite of your busy work schedule and family commitments, block out some time to be with the Lord. You may not be able to take as much time as you would like but you can start with what time you have. I recommend starting with a clean slate. Do not begin with where you are and the problems you currently face. Go back to your salvation and remember how God saved you. Think about what you were thinking and how you felt. Take time to thank the Lord for saving you.

Then take some time to remember when God called you to serve Him. You cannot forget your call. It is impossible not to remember what you were doing and how you felt when you heard His voice. Do you remember what He said? Do you recall how you felt or what you said in reply to Him? Were you afraid like Moses? Did you feel unworthy like Isaiah? Did fire burn in your bones like Jeremiah or did the Kingdom come alive like it did for John the Baptist?

Your calling is often the thing that keeps you in the ministry that God has for you when everything around you screams for you to quit and run away.

In addition to these two things, I like to remember the times when God worked in my life in great ways. I like to remember sermons that moved people, decisions I made that helped churches grow, and crucial times when God gave me wisdom, protection, and victory over enemies and obstacles that threatened me and my ministry. I like to remember the times God delivered me from things beyond my control. I also like to think about those special times when the Holy Spirit opened up my mind to things in Scripture that changed my life.

We all have those things in our past, insuring that we will have them in the future. God has great plans for us and trusting Him insures that we will see those plans come to life. As hard as the struggle is right now, however long the road stretches before us, and whatever the sacrifices we must make, He will see those plans to fulfillment. Our task is to trust, obey, and work until He tells us to stop.

Moses never made it into the Promised Land but God's people did. They entered as a new nation fully equipped and prepared to live in that land God had given them. Moses did his job despite disappointments, detours, setbacks, and personal failures. So will you. You will finish your journey if you truly believe God has saved you and called you to be a leader for Him. There are and there will be days we would rather not have and there are days of victory and breakthrough to enjoy. The days themselves are not our final measurement. The compilation of those days is what counts. Today are you faithful to Him who has saved and called you? If not, then make it right and get back into the work of the Kingdom.

Don't wait for the right time to lead. Now is the time and you are the one, the only one, who can lead your people. You cannot lead anyone else's so lead yours. Take courage from your King and do His business today. No leader is made instantly. It takes years and years of experiences, failures, and victories to get there.

So get started and who knows, in forty years or so, you may reach your leadership peak.

A Final Word

———◈◈◈———

I truly hope this book has been a good read for you. Often I read someone I do not know and I find myself wondering why he or she wrote something I do not agree with or understand. This has likely happened to you, so I want to add something that is important to me and I hope will encourage you.

I am a pastor having served in ministry for over forty years. I have made many, many mistakes as a leader; some from ignorance, some from pride, some from inexperience, and many from haste. One mistake I hope to avoid for the years that I have left as a Kingdom leader is the mistake of not developing as a leader. Moses encourages me to keep leading, learning, and developing. When I have to lay my tasks aside, I hope that I am at my best as a leader. I have a passion to make Christ known, to see persons surrender their lives in faith to Him as Savior and Lord, to see them mature in Him, and to equip them to serve Him. That is a biblical vision I have worked on all my leadership life and I haven't perfected it yet—but I'm trying.

If you have been encouraged and motivated to develop as a leader, I have succeeded. If you are resolved to stay at your task in spite of its dangers and difficulties, I have succeeded. If you have returned to your salvation and calling and come away stronger as a leader, I have succeeded. If your passion for the Father, Christ, and the Holy Spirit has increased and you are willing to go where He sends, stay where He wills, say what He speaks, and do what He shows you, I have succeeded.

I count it the highest privilege to be in ministry to announce the Good News and to join Christ as He builds His Church (and churches) and expands His Kingdom. One day we will all meet in eternity to joyfully discuss our times on Earth and what God did through us. Until that day, I am glad to be counted with you as one of God's leaders, working hard to fulfill His purposes.

May God bless you as He finds you always abounding in the work of the Lord.

Gene Mims
Nashville, Tennessee

Appendix

—⊲*∾*⊳—

28 Leadership Principles

1. It takes a long time to become a great leader.

2. Personal failures do not mean the end of our leadership.

3. God never calls us to anything small or insignificant.

4. God is constantly working in the world to establish His purposes and He works through leaders to accomplish these purposes.

5. God's call is usually to something that is beyond our background, experience, training, skill, education, and comfort level.

6. A person's age does not determine what God can do through him or her.

7. God's call comes with His power and authority which He gives us to exercise.

8. Great leaders get better by listening to wisdom and truth from others.

9. Great leaders do not give up on their people.

10. Great leaders teach to transform people.

11. You cannot lead people where you have not gone or are unwilling to go.

12. Choose persons to help you wisely. If you must, choose character over skills.

13. Whatever God has called you to, you can do with the people you have right now.

14. Your skills may take you where your character cannot keep you.

15. Godly character cannot be defeated.

16. Great leaders do what God wants, teach what they learn from Him, go where He sends, and do not initiate anything without His permission.

17. The way a leader speaks about people, especially his parents, reveals much about his character.

18. Great leaders are and remain sexually pure.

19. Great leaders do not lie, ever.

20. Great leaders are humble and persistent.

21. Great leaders communicate clear messages over and over and over...

22. Great leaders meet opposition with strength of character and the power of their calling and vision.

23. Time alone with the Lord is the key to good relationships.

24. Most of a leader's problems are people problems.

25. You cannot reach the delights of your vision until you meet the demands of your problems.

26. Great leaders do the difficult task of developing visions and strategies and the tedious work of handling the details of the work that needs to be done.

27. Great leaders have the privilege of building great friendships without compromising their role of working with God to build His Kingdom.

28. Your calling is often what keeps you in the ministry God has for you when everything around you screams for you to quit and run away.